Getting the Most from Predictable Books

Strategies and Activities
for Teaching with More than
75 Favorite Children's Books

by

Michael F. Opitz

SCHOLASTIC
PROFESSIONAL **B**OOKS

New York • Toronto • London • Auckland • Sydney

Acknowledgements

I am greatly indebted to several individuals who helped in the preparation of this manuscript: to my many students and mentors through whom I have learned much about the teaching of reading and writing; to Terry Cooper, Editor-in-Chief, Scholastic Professional Books, for providing me with the opportunity and space to create; to Helen Moore Sorvillo, Editor, Scholastic Professional Books, for her insights, but especially for making the task an enjoyable one. And, for her on-going support in every conceivable way, I thank Sheryl, my first lady.

Cover design by Vincent Ceci and Frank Maiocco
Book design and diagrams by Carmen Robert Sorvillo
Illustrations by James Graham Hale
Copyright © 1995 by Michael F. Opitz
Printed in USA

12 11 10 9 8 7 6 5 4   7 8 9/9
ISBN 0-590-27049-4

Table of Contents

About This Book

The primary purpose of this book is to provide a resource of over 800 predictable trade books, along with suggestions for their use. In Part I you'll find some definitions of terms associated with predictable literature. You'll also find some specific reasons and suggestions for using and innovating on predictable books as well as ideas for ways to use this book.

Part II opens with matrices that show the featured authors and their books along with the predictable characteristics of each. Three "Book Bursts," which include an annotation, a suggested way to innovate on a given text, and cross-curricular activities are provided for nearly every letter of the alphabet. These activities are just a start — You will likely think of additional appropriate activities to use with the books. Following each set of Book Bursts is an alphabetical bibliography of additional predictable literature authors and their books.

Sample text sets are next: these show one way to group books around a given topic while providing for individual differences. Common questions and concerns about the use of predictable literature are then listed along with references that can be used to address each issue. You'll also find a listing of commercial programs that make use of predictable books.

This book highlights trade books that are predictable rather than books that have been written for a reading program. There is a big difference here!

Predictable trade books, that is, books that we can purchase in bookstores and check out of our local libraries, communicate information — in one form or another. The books come in various sizes and are illustrated in a variety of ways. These illustrations often provide the reader with helpful clues. Often the authors of these books unknowingly use features that make the book easy for the beginning or the older less fluent reader to read. In fact, these features lend so much support that the reader can use what is known about language, memory, and life experiences to predict what the author has written and join in the reading class during the first reading of the book. Make no mistake, however. The thoughts these authors want to convey remain as the focus.

In the commercially prepared programs listed on page 110, however, the opposite sometimes occurs. The books that comprise these programs are often written intentionally using specific language features. While the authors also convey information to a given audience, they are also concerned with using certain language features, and having their books increase in difficulty so that gradually the student becomes an independent reader without relying on language features and illustrations. More often than not the books are the same size and line drawings and/or photographs are used to illustrate them.

My main goal is to help children become independent, life-long readers of trade books.

Both types of books are valuable and I recommend using both. My main goal is to help children become independent, life-long readers of *trade books*, readers who choose to read for a variety of purposes; those who can and do use the library. My experience in working with countless beginning readers and their teachers is that this is not likely to happen if we rely totally on commercial programs. This is the case because students come to see themselves as readers of "those books," rarely realizing that there is a world of other books in the library within their reach.

To best accomplish the goal, students need to be exposed to trade books for reading. They also need to be told they are reading— "You're reading now," I often say to a child who has just read a predictable trade book. "I read the whole book by myself," the child responds. "Guess what?" I say. "There are several others in our library you can read, too!" The looks on their faces, the joy expressed by their broad smiles, as it dawns on them that, yes, they can read, that they're "in the club!" is exhilarating— for both reader and teacher!

- Michael F. Opitz

Part I:
Definitions, Reasons, and Suggestions

Definitions

What are predictable books?

Predictable books are books written with specific features that enable children to read with ease. The books enable children to use what they know about language, memory, and life experiences to predict the words coming up in the text, thus the name *predictable books*. The characteristics? *Predictable* books have . . .

📖   **pictures that support the text** such as those used in Butterworth's *Busy People*. These pictures help the reader figure out what the text might say;

📖   **a repeated sentence or phrase** such as "Just like Daddy" in Asche's book with a like title;

📖   **the use of rhyme and rhythm** such as the rhyming pattern used in Fox's *Time for Bed*;

📖   **a cumulative pattern** in which a sentence is repeated and the story is added onto such as in Aardema's *Bringing the Rain to Kapiti Plain*;

📖   **familiar cultural sequences or storylines** such as days of the week, counting, or familiar events as in Falwell's *Feast for 10*.

Often these characteristics, or features, overlap as the matrices on pages 15 to 17 illustrate. Notice, for example, that rhyme, rhythm, repetition, and a familiar storyline are used in Anholt's *Kids*.

Some predictable books have been enlarged into *big books*. The terms *big* and *predictable* are sometimes used synonomously. *Shared reading* is the process the teacher and children use as they read and re-read a book together.

What does it mean to innovate on the text?

Like the terms *big book* and *shared reading*, *innovation* is a term often associated with predictable literature. Basically, it involves using the basic structure used by the author along with one's original words to create another text. Carle's *Have You Seen My Cat?*, for example, might become *Have You Seen My Bird?* Why have children innovate on text? See pages 9 and 10!

Seven Good Reasons
for Using Predictable Literature

1. From the very start, children perceive themselves as readers. Because they feel successful from the start, they are more likely to want to do it again.

2. Children read whole books. A positive spinoff is that they learn to read by reading and begin to develop independence immediately.

3. Children see that reading must make sense. Consequently, children grasp an accurate perception of reading — understanding!

4. Children see that reading is an enjoyable activity. With predictable literature, children are able to use their memory, what they know about the language, and picture clues as they read along with the others. Although they may not be able to identify any single word, this role playing or "pretend reading" is a start. They'll grow with teacher guidance.

5. Children see that books are often read more than once. Because they experience success with the reading, children have a desire to read the book again, which is exactly what experienced readers do with good books!

6. Predictable books provide a meaningful context for instructional purposes. Predictable books can be used to teach many skills and strategies, such as using several cues to gain meaning and to check one's predictions. The books can also be used to teach oral reading fluency, sight vocabulary, letters, story structure, and comprehension skills such as sequencing and prediction.

7. They enable the teacher to provide for individual differences.
Regardless of "level," all children have real books they can read. This reinforces the idea that everyone can read something. Likewise, within a shared reading experience, children who are just learning to read can learn from the others without feeling embarrassed.

In essence, then, using predictable books can be viewed much like a circular plot to create independent, life-long readers as "The Because Circle" shown below illustrates.

Six Good Reasons for Innovating on Text

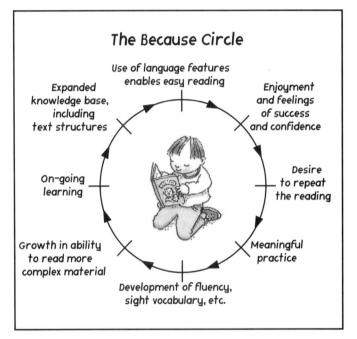

The Because Circle

Use of language features enables easy reading

Expanded knowledge base, including text structures

Enjoyment and feelings of success and confidence

On-going learning

Desire to repeat the reading

Growth in ability to read more complex material

Meaningful practice

Development of fluency, sight vocabulary, etc.

1. To help children to experience the joy of being an author. Children are encouraged to write within a supportive structure, and become able to write with ease. They see that writing can be fun — something they can and want to do. They perceive themselves as writers.

2. To help children to learn about language. Innovating encourages children to play around with the language. They learn about their language by using it to create.

3. To help children to develop knowledge of print. Children learn about letters, sounds, syllables, and words. They have to apply what they know about all of these language features when writing. If you want effective phonics, spelling and word instruction, here it is!

4. To help children to see that books and stories have structures.
When students create their own books, they become aware of components like the title page and dedication page. They also come to see that stories are written with certain structures. Understanding of text structure leads to better reading comprehension!

5. To provide children with additional books they enjoy reading both at school and at home. Children often create their own books when they innovate on a text. Sometimes these books are placed in the classroom or school library, other times these books are taken home, where they provide interesting reading material so children will practice reading.

6. To help children to move beyond memorization. True, memory is helpful to all readers, but it is especially helpful for those just beginning and/or those older less fluent readers. However, in the long run, memory isn't enough. Students need to go beyond it if they are to develop into able readers and writers. Creating their own texts within a supportive framework, then, is one way to help them move beyond memorization.

Having provided these reasons, a reminder is in order. Innovation provides a *temporary* support. One way we can guard against it becoming a meaningless fill-in-the-blank exercise is to have children use the basic structure to create books for reading rather than worksheets to be tossed. Another way is to provide the structure and allow the children to decide whether or not they would like to use it. The structure can be regarded as a support that children can discard when they feel it's no longer needed.

Suggestions for Successful Text Innovations

To be successful when innovating on text, children need to know the original text well. Here are some suggestions that apply to the use of big books and regular-sized versions of the book. Completing this suggested sequence may take more than one day.

Before Reading

1. Gather the children.
> You might say: "Come to our story area. I have a story to share with you!"

2. Read the title.
> Point to each word, and have the children look at the cover.
> "Take a look at the cover. The words say . . ."

3. Ask what they think.

Tell the children that you will be writing some of their ideas about what might happen. "Just by looking at the picture and hearing the title of the book, what do you think will happen? I'm going to write down some of your predictions in a chart."

During Reading

1. Read the story without stopping.

This enables the children to enjoy the story and conveys the idea that understanding is essential. "I'm going to read the whole story without stopping so that you can see what it's about."

2. Read the book again.

Point to the words as you read. Invite students to join you when they want. (Like choral reading.) "Let's take another look at this book. This time I need your help. When you want, you may join in."

3. Do a third reading.

Assign parts of the class to read certain parts of the story. "I have an idea! Let's have all of you on this side read the part that says . . . . The rest of you read the part that says . . . . "

After Reading

1. Discuss what happened.

Revisit their predictions. "Let's take a look at the chart we made before we read the story for the first time. Were any of our predictions correct?"

2. Act it out.

Use simple props. After giving them parts, reread or retell the story (or have students who didn't get a part in the first reading do so). Children with parts perform at the appropriate part of the story. "Now that we've read this story several times, let's act it out. We'll have this circle of chairs be our stage. When we retell the story, you need to come into the circle when the name of the character you're playing is mentioned."

3. Innovate on the text.

"This story has been about a polar bear. Let's use another animal's name to begin the story." Listed below are ways to have children innovate on text. (If children are new to the idea, you might want to do a class innovation to start using one of the first three suggestions.)

📖   If you are using a big book, you can use sticky-notes to cover given words. As the children suggest new words, simply write them on the sticky-notes.

📖   Present the basic structure on an overhead transparency with deleted words. Have children fill in possible words.

📖   If you are using a regular-sized version of the story, print it on a large chart or on sentence strips that you place in a pocket chart. Cover the words you want students to change, either with sticky-notes or index cards. As above, write the words the children suggest. Then have them read the "new" story.

📖   Have students create an entire book using a given structure. You would want to have some blank paper or paper with the basic structure printed on it stapled together in book form. Students then create their own sentences and illustrate each to create their own books.

📖   Have each student contribute a single page to a class book. Each child would be expected to come up with one sentence and an illustration for it. Once the book is assembled, the class could do a reading of it. You might also want to make a copy of the book for each student. These single pages could also be hung around the room in a given sequence creating a "wall story" for students to read.

📖   You might decide that you would like to have students work in pairs to complete a given page to be compiled into a class book. Both students could work on the writing and the illustration.

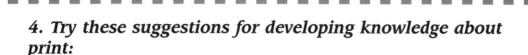

4. Try these suggestions for developing knowledge about print:

📖 Print each sentence of the story on a sentence strip. Place these strips in a pocket holder and have students read the story with you. Then scramble the sentence strips by distributing them to your students. Have them rebuild the story in the chart. Beginning with a repetitive story would guarantee success.

📖 If you want to have your students focus on words, distribute given words to students and have them place their word card over the word shown in the sentence.

📖 If you want to have your students focus on letters, give each a letter card and have them match it to a letter shown in the pocket chart story.

Text Sets

Using the annotated books and the additional bibliographies, develop "text sets." Text sets are sets of books related to a common element or theme, as shown on page 107. For example, you might want to develop a text set for friendship. You could search the matrices shown on pages 15, 16 and 17, bibliographies, and Book Bursts for books that relate to this topic. Once located, you could use these books in several ways:

📖 Obtain several copies of one title, enough for a given group of students to read. The book could then be used during a guided reading lesson, one in which you help guide the students through their reading of the text.

📖 Locate several copies of four or five different titles that correspond to the theme. Allow children to select the title they would like to read. Once selected, you could group the children with like titles or children with four different titles for a guided reading lesson. Another way to use these text sets would be to have students read their chosen selection and then have like titles get together to note the most important ideas. These ideas could then be shared with others in the class. After having children share their books, you could discuss how the books relate to the theme.

Gather several titles related to the theme and let children select the title they would like to read. After reading, have students pair up and talk about their books – how they are alike and different. This is an especially effective way to meet the diverse needs of your students yet keep them focused on the same theme.

More Ideas

1. Choose several variations of the same title.

For example, you could use Nodset's *Who Took the Farmer's Hat?* shown on page 70 and Van Laan's *This Is the Hat* shown on page 93. Either read to them or have children read the variations. Once the two versions have been read, do a comparison-contrast activity to note how they are alike and different. You might want to do this on an enlarged matrix. Write the titles down the left side of the matrix, the attributes along the top. Then have children put a dot next to the titles that have the given attributes. Likenesses and differences will become obvious as students look at the completed matrix.

2. Use this bibliography to create a predictable book section in your classroom, school, and/or public library.

A "Predictable Literature" sign could lead students to the section. NOTE: Because predictable books are not necessarily the same as "Easy Readers," books often written with controlled vocabulary, special type, and standard format, a separate section for predictable literature is warranted. Older less fluent readers are better able to "save face" and are more inclined to go to a section entitled "Predictable Literature."

3. Do an author study.

Choose books written by the same author. Have children read the various titles and discuss the author's style.

Part II: The Books

Author and Title	date published	rhyme / rhythm	repetition	cumulative	circular plot	familiar sequence
Aker, S. *What Comes in 2's, 3's, and 4's?*	93		●			●
Anholt, Catherine & Laurence *Kids*	92	●	●			●
Ayres, P. *Guess What?*	87	●				●
Brown, C. *City Sounds*	92		●			
Brown, M. *The Important Book*	49		●			
Butterworth, N. *Busy People*	86		●			
Cameron, A. *The Cat Sat on the Mat*	94		●			
Carle, E. *Have You Seen My Cat?*	87		●			
Curtis, J. *When I Was Little*	93		●			●
Dodd, A. *Footprints and Shadows*	92		●			●
Dragonwagon, C. *Alligator Arrived with Apples*	92	●				
Dunbar, J. *Seven Sillies*	93			●		
Ekker, E. *What Is Beyond the Hill?*	85		●			
Ets, M. *Elephant in a Well*	72		●	●		
Evans, K. *Hunky Dory Ate It*	92	●	●			●
Falwell, C. *Feast for 10*	93	●				●
Fleming, D. *Barnyard Banter*	94		●			
Fox, M. *Time for Bed*	93	●				
Gackenback, D. *Supposes*	89		●			
Gomi, T. *Who Hid It?*	91		●			
Guarino, D. *Is Your Mama a Llama?*	89	●	●			

Author and Title

Author and Title	date published	rhyme / rhythm	repetition	cumulative	circular plot	familiar sequence
Halsey, M. *Jump for Joy: A Book of Months*	94	●				●
Harshman, M. *Only One*	93		●			●
Hutchins, P. *My Best Friend*	93		●			●
Inkpen, M. *Billy's Beetle*	91			●		
Isadora, R. *I See*	85		●			●
Janovitz, M. *Is It Time?*	94	●	●	●		●
Johnson, R. *Look at Me in Funny Clothes!*	94		●			
Jonas, A. *Now We Can Go*	86					●
Koontz, R. *I See Something You Don't See*	92	●	●			
Krall, V. *New Friends, True Friends, Stuck-Like-Glue Friends*	94	●				●
Kuskin, K. *City Noise*	94	●				
Lankford, M. *Is It Dark? Is It Light?*	91		●	●		
Lindbergh, R. *What Is the Sun?*	94	●	●			
Loban, A. *Away from Home*	94	●				
Martin, B. *Polar Bear, Polar Bear, What Do You Hear?*	91	●	●	●		
McDonnell, F. *I Love Animals*	94		●			
Miranda, A. *Does a Mouse Have a House?*	94	●				
Neitzel, S. *The Jacket I Wear in the Snow*	89	●	●	●		
Nerlove, M. *If All the World Were Paper*	91	●	●			
Nodset, J. *Who Took the Farmer's Hat?*	63		●			
O'Keefe, S. *One Hungry Monster*	89	●				●
Ormerod, J. *101 Things to Do with a Baby*	84		●			
Oxenbury, H. *It's My Birthday*	93	●	●	●		●
Paschkis, J. *So Sleepy, Wide Awake*	94	●			●	
Phillips, L. *The Upside Down Riddle Book*	82	●				
Protopopescu, O. *The Perilous Pit*	93				●	

Author and Title

Author and Title	date published	rhyme / rhythm	repetition	cumulative	circular plot	familiar sequence
Roe, E. *All I Am*	90		●			
Rogers, A. *Yellow Hippo*	90		●			
Rogers, P. *What Will the Weather Be Like Today?*	89	●				●
Schindel, J. *What's for Lunch?*	94		●	●		
Stevenson, J. *Fun, No Fun*	94		●			●
Stolz, M. *Say Something*	93		●			
Tedesco, D. *Do You Know How Much I Love You?*	94	●		●		
Titherington, J. *Pumpkin, Pumpkin*	86		●	●		●
Tofts, H. *I Wish*	94	●	●			
Udry, J. *A Tree Is Nice*	56		●			
Van Laan, N. *This Is the Hat*	92	●	●	●		
Vipont, E. *The Elephant and the Bad Baby*	69		●	●		
Wellington, M. *The Sheep Follow*	92		●		●	
Wildsmith, B. & R. *Look Closer*	93		●			
Williams, S. *I Went Walking*	90	●	●			
Yolen, J. *Old Dame Counterpane*	94	●	●		●	
Yoshi *Who's Hiding Here?*	87	●	●			
Young, R. *Who Says Moo?*	94	●	●			
Ziefert, H. *Where Is my Baby?*	94		●			
Zolotow, C. *This Quiet Lady*	92		●			

Aker, Suzanne

What Comes in 2's, 3's, and 4's?

Illustrated by Bernie Karlin
Simon & Schuster, 1993. ISBN: 0-671-67173-1

Annotation

This book introduces the numbers *2*, *3*, and *4* by showing specific objects in everyday life. The body is used to introduce *2*, a traffic signal for *3*, and the four seasons for *4*. Several other pictures are provided for each number. Each illustration is labeled to tie the book together. Although it has a story feel, this book could also be considered informational.

Innovation

Brainstorm with students other objects that show *2*, *3*, or *4*. Use the basic question shown at the right and one of the suggestions listed on pages 12 and 13 to create additional books for other numbers. Drawings, magazine pictures, photographs, or any combination of these could be used for illustrations.

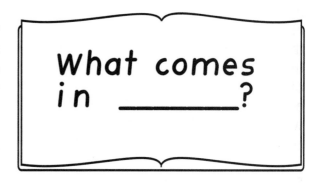

Cross-Curricular Activities

Science: Invite students to go on a scavenger hunt around the room, school, or on a neighborhood walk looking for objects that represent a given number. Each student could be given a clipboard and asked to make a list of their discoveries.

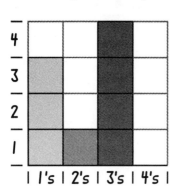

Mathematics: Once back in the classroom, construct a bar graph which shows the numbers that were being scavenged. One space is colored in for each item found that represents that number. Use the graph to teach one or more of the following concepts: more than, less than, equal, same as, addition, subtraction. This can be accomplished by having students look at the graph to answer specific questions such as: "Which number has the most? the least? How many would we have to add to the 2's column to make it equal the 3's column?"

Anholt, Catherine & Laurence

Kids

Illustrated by the authors
Candlewick Press, 1992. ISBN: 1-56402-097-5

Annotation

Just what do kids most often do? What are some things they like? This book answers several questions such as these, helping students better understand themselves and their likenesses and differences.

Innovation

Invite children to discuss what they like to do and don't like to do, noting any likenesses and differences to those stated in the text. Use the basic questions shown at the right and one of the suggestions listed on pages 12 and 13 to create additional books. In fact, you could also replace *kids* with other words, such as, *grownups*, *mothers*, *fathers*, *brothers*, or *teachers*.

What do kids ___?
What do ___ ___?

Cross-Curricular Activities

Mathematics: You might want to use graphing to focus in on one likeness and difference. For example, you could make a bar graph that shows lunch pails on one column, paper sacks on a second, and home on a third. Give each student a small piece of paper to paste into the column that represents how lunch is brought to school or if they go home for lunch. Once all have had a chance to respond, ask students to note likenesses and differences.

Social Studies: Give each student a piece of paper that contains a Venn diagram. Divide the children into pairs and ask them to fill out their diagrams with their partner. Each writes his/her name below one side of the diagram, which is where their differences are recorded. Likenesses are recorded in the overlapping circles. Students will most likely start with the obvious features such as that they both have two eyes (listed in the center of overlapping circles) but that their eye colors are different (listed on their representative sides). The more they get to know one another, less obvious features such as interests and favorite foods may surface.

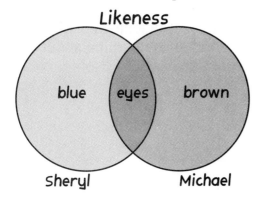

Likeness

blue   eyes   brown

Sheryl   Michael

Ayres, Pam

Guess What?

Illustrated by Julie Lacome
Knopf, 1987. ISBN: 0-394-89287-9

Annotation

Children who like guessing games will enjoy using the clues to answer the questions stated in this book. One page shows a character with objects and the reader is asked, "What will _____ do?" After using the clues provided in the picture, a turn of the page reveals the answer.

Innovation

Review all of the characters in the book, what they did, and what they needed to complete their job. Use the pattern shown at the right and one of the suggestions listed on pages 12 and 13 to create additional books.

_____ has _____
and _____, too.
What is _____
about to do?

Cross-Curricular Activities

Language Arts: To further develop students' speaking abilities, have students use the list to compose an oral riddle for a given activity. For example, "You need red, pink, and white paper to create me. People feel good when they get me on a special day. What am I?" (valentine)

Home	School	Vacation
Swimming Reading	Reading	Skiing Swimming Reading

Mathematics: Make a list of categories of activities such as recreational, school-related, and vacation-related. Have children list types of activities associated with each category. When activities overlap, have them write the name of the activity in each category.

Social Studies: Discuss various occupations with your students and what tools workers need to best complete their jobs. This might coincide with learning about community helpers. Make a list of the various occupations and their required tools.

Additional A's

Aardema, Verna. *Bringing the Rain to Kapiti Plain*. New York: Scholastic, 1981.

Abisch, Roz. *Around the House That Jack Built*. New York: Parents' Press, 1972.

Accorsi, William. *Billy's Button*. New York: Greenwillow, 1992.

Ada, Alma. *The Gold Coin*. New York: Macmillan, 1991.

Adams, Ken. *When I Was Your Age*. Barron's, 1992.

Adams, Pam. *There Was an Old Lady Who Swallowed a Fly*. Child's Play International, 1990.

Adoff, Arnold. *The Cabbages Are Chasing the Rabbits*. New York: Harcourt Brace, 1985.

Ahlberg, Janet and Allen. *Each Peach Pear Plum*. New York: Scholastic, 1978.

Alain. *One, Two, Three, Going to Sea*. New York: Scholastic, 1964.

Alborough, Jez. *Hide and Seek*. Cambridge, MA: Candlewick, 1993.

——. *Where's My Teddy?* Cambridge, MA: Candlewick, 1992.

Alda, Arlene. *Pig, Horse, or Cow, Don't Wake Me Now*. New York: Bantam/Doubleday, 1994.

Alexander, Lloyd. *Fortune Tellers*. New York: Dutton, 1992.

Aliki. *We Are Best Friends*. New York: Mulberry, 1987.

——. *At Mary Bloom's*. New York: Greenwillow, 1976.

——. *Go Tell Aunt Rhody*. New York: Macmillan, 1974.

——. *June 7!* New York: Macmillan, 1972.

——. *Hush Little Baby*. Englewood Cliffs, NJ: Prentice-Hall, 1968.

Alger, Leclaire. *Always Room for One More*. Holt, 1965.

——. *All in the Morning Early*. New York: Holt, 1963.

Allbright, Viv. *Ten Go Hopping*. Faber, 1985.

Allen, Pamela. *Bertie and the Bear*. New York: Coward-McCann, 1984.

——. *Who Sank the Boat?* New York: Coward-McCann, 1982.

Allen, Marjorie. *Changes*. New York: Macmillan, 1991.

Anholt, Catherine and Laurence. *All About You*. New York: Scholastic, 1991.

——. *What I Like*. New York: Putnam, 1991.

Appleby, Ellen. *The Three Billy-Goats Gruff*. New York: Scholastic, 1984.

Archambault, John, and Bill Martin, Jr. *A Beautiful Feast for a Big King Cat*. New York: Harper Collins, 1989.

Arnold, Tedd. *No Jumping on the Bed*. New York: Scholastic, 1987.

Asch, Frank. *Happy Birthday, Moon*. New York: Scholastic, 1982.

——. *Just Like Daddy*. New York: Simon & Schuster, 1981.

——. *Monkey Face*. New York: Parents' Magazine, 1977.

Aylesworth, Jim. *My Son John*. New York: Henry Holt, 1994.

——. *The Completed Hickory-Dickory Dock*. New York: Aladdin, 1994.

——. *Old Black Fly*. New York: Henry Holt, 1992.

——. *One Crow: A Counting Rhyme*. New York: Harper, 1988.

——. *Mary's Mirror*. New York: Holt, 1982.

——. *Tonight's the Night*. Chicago: Whitman, 1981.

Ayres, Pam. *Guess Where?* Cambridge, MA: Candlewick, 1994.

Brown, Craig
City Sounds

Illustrated by the author
Greenwillow, 1992. ISBN: 0-688-10028-7

Annotation

A farmer goes to the post office in the big city to pick up a special delivery. He hears sounds of the city that are quite different from those he hears in the country. He decides to return to his farm where he can open his package containing baby chicks and listen to them peep. This is an excellent book to use for developing intonation because of the text type.

Innovation

Ask children what sounds they hear when they go to the city and what objects make those sounds. Use the basic sentence shown at the right and one of the suggestions on pages 12 and 13 to create another book. Perhaps students could be taken to a farm and create a "sounds of the farm" book upon their return. If so, the book might start with, "We went to the farm and here's what we heard..." The page shown here could then be used. "We went on a walk and this is what we heard..." might be another way to begin the book.

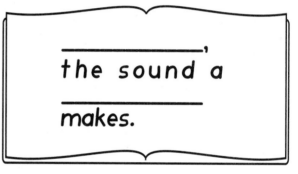

_____, the sound a _____ makes.

Cross-Curricular Activities

Science/Health: The farmer used one of his senses when he went to the city. How about the other senses? Have students state things they could taste, touch and see in the city. Perhaps their ideas could be written on cards that are placed on a chart labeled for each sense.

	Sight	Touch	Smell	Taste	Hearing
1. Cars	x	x			x
2. Bakery	x		x		
3.					

Mathematics: Ask students to categorize by giving them a matrix. Down the left hand side are ideas generated in the idea stated above. The five senses are listed across the top. Students look at the item on the left and place an X under each sense that could be used to learn about the object. This activity lends itself to working in small groups or pairs.

Brown, Margaret Wise
The Important Book

Illustrated by Leonard Weisgard
Harper & Row, 1949. ISBN: 0-06-020720-5

Annotation

What's important? This book tells you. Each page opens with the naming of an object. Features describing the object are then given with a statement of the most important characteristic at the end of the page. The book closes by celebrating the uniqueness of individuals as Brown writes, "the important thing about you is that you are you!"

Innovation

Have students name things that are important to them or recall some of those items mentioned in the book. Using the frame shown below and one of the suggestions mentioned on pages 12 and 13, invite students to create.

> The important thing about ___ is ___.
> It is _____.
> It is _____.
> It is _____.
> But the important thing about _____
> is that it is _____.

Cross-Curricular Activities

Social Studies: This book lends itself to a beginning of the year ice breaker. Ask students to think of things that describe themselves and what they consider to be their most important attribute. They could then fill out the frame shown above and share it with the class. You could also have students interview one another, fill out the form on the person they interviewed, and introduce that person to the rest of the class by reading the form.

Language Arts: You also might want to use this book to teach about main idea and supporting details and writing paragraphs. Students could choose a topic and list a distinguishing characteristic. They could then list details that supported the main idea in paragraph form. A variation of this would be to have students use this form to complete a "mini report" on a state bird, flower, flag, animal, or person.

Butterworth, Nick

Busy People

Illustrated by the author
Candlewick, 1986. ISBN: 1-56402-365-6

Annotation

Who are the workers in our community? What are the things they use to do their jobs? The answers to these two questions provide the content of this book. The name and occupation of the person are stated and a picture showing the required tools are shown on facing pages. A variety of occupations are assigned to both males and females, illustrating that people can be what they want to be.

Innovation

Review the many occupations listed in the book. You might want to have students share what their parents do. Use the frame shown here and the suggestions provided on pages 12 and 13 to have students create a related book.

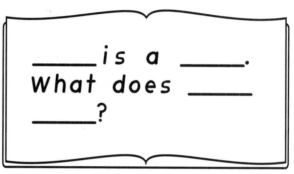

Cross-Curricular Activities

The Arts: This book can be used to develop comprehension and self-expression. On cards write or draw each occupation mentioned in the book and put the cards in a paper bag. In turn, have students draw out a card and pantomime the occupation shown on the card.

Language Arts: To further students' abilities to ask questions and make statements, follow the directions above. However, blindfold the student taking a card out of the bag. Show the chosen card to the rest of the class. Next, tape the card to the blindfolded person's back. Remove the blindfold and instruct the student to ask questions to discover the occupation taped on his/her back. After asking the question, the class responds in unison in a complete sentence such as, "Yes, you do use that tool." The amount of clues provided will vary as will the amount of time you want to have the student try.

Additional *B*'s

Bacon, Ron. *Wind*. New York: Scholastic, 1984.

Baer, Gene. *Thump Rat a Tat Tat*. New York: Harper & Row, 1989.

Baker, Keith. *Hide and Snake*. New York: Harcourt Brace, 1991.

——. *Who is This Beast?* New York: Voyager/Harcourt Brace, 1990.

Balian, Lorna. *The Animal*. New York: Abington Press, 1972.

——. *Where in the World Is Henry?* Scarsdale, NJ: Bradbury Press, 1972.

Bang, Molly. *Yellow Ball*. New York: Puffin, 1991.

Barchas, Sarah. *I Was Walking Down the Road*. New York: Scholastic, 1975.

Barton, Bryon. *Buzz Buzz Buzz*. New York: Scholastic, 1973.

Barrett, Judi. *I'm Too Small, You're Too Big*. New York: Atheneum, 1981.

——. *Animals Should Definitely Not Act Like People*. New York: Atheneum, 1980.

——. *Animals Should Definitely Not Wear Clothing*. New York: Atheneum, 1977.

Baum, Arline & Joseph Baum. *One Bright Monday Morning*. New York: Random House, 1962.

Bauman, A. F. *Guess Where You're Going, Guess What You'll Do?* Boston: Houghton Mifflin, 1989.

Bauer, Caroline Feller. *My Mom Travels A Lot*. New York: Warne, 1981.

Baylor, Byrd. *Guess Who My Favorite Person Is?* New York: Scribner, 1977.

Bayton, Martin. *Why Do You Love Me?* New York: Greenwillow, 1988.

Becker, John. *Seven Little Rabbits*. New York: Scholastic, 1973.

Beckman, Kaj. *Lisa Cannot Sleep*. New York: Franklin Watts, 1969.

Benjamin, Alan. *Buck*. New York: Simon and Schuster, 1993.

Blake, Quentin. *All Join In*. Boston: Little Brown, 1990.

Blocksma, Mary. *The Best Dressed Bear*. Chicago: Children's Press, 1984.

Blos, Joan. *A Seed, a Flower, a Minute, an Hour*. Half Moon, 1992.

Borden, Louise. *Caps, Hats, Socks, & Mittens*. New York: Scholastic, 1989.

Brandenberg, Franz. *A Robber, a Robber*. New York: Greenwillow, 1976.

——. *I Wish I Was Sick, Too*. New York: Greenwillow, 1976.

Brown, Margaret Wise. *Goodnight Moon*. New York: Harper & Row, 1947.

Brown, Ruth. *A Dark, Dark Tale*. New York: Dial, 1981.

——. *Ladybug, Ladybug*. New York: Dutton, 1988.

Buchanan, Joan. *It's a Good Thing*. Toronto: Annick Press, 1984.

Buckley, Helen E. *Grandfather and I*. New York: Lothrop, Lee & Shepard, 1959.

Bulla, Clyde Robert. *The Chalk Box Kid*. New York: Random House, 1987.

Buller, Jon & Susan Schade. *I Love You, Good Night*. Simon & Schuster, 1988.

Bunting, Eve. *Flower Garden*. New York: Harcourt Brace, 1994.

——. *Red Fox Running*. New York: Clarion, 1993.

Burningham, John. *Would You Rather?* New York: Crowell, 1978.

——. Mr. *Grumpy's Outing*. New York: Holt, 1970.

Burton, Marilee. *One Little Chickadee*. New York: Tambourine, 1994.

——. *Tail Toes Eyes Ears Nose*. New York: Harper Trophy, 1988.

Butler, Dorothy. *My Brown Bear Barney*. New York: Greenwillow, 1988.

Butler, Stephen. *The Mouse and the Apple*. New York: Tambourine Books, 1994.

Byars, Betsy. *Hooray for the Golly Sisters!* New York: Harper & Row, 1990.

Cameron, Alice
The Cat Sat on the Mat

Illustrated by Carl Jones
Houghton Mifflin, 1994. ISBN: 0-395-68392-0

Annotation

The family cat sits on the mat outside, waiting to be let in when the family gets home. Once inside, he gets into all kinds of mischief by sitting on things he shouldn't. This mischief is exactly what enables the cat to finish the story where it started – outside on the mat! The book is designed so that the reader can peek through the center of the page and try to guess what the cat is sitting on. The words "The cat sat on the. . ." entice readers to turn the page to see if their predictions were correct.

Innovation

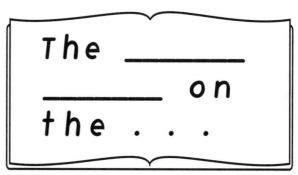

Suggest other family pets that might get into trouble by misbehaving. Ask students to create their own "guess" books using the pattern in the book and substituting the name of the animal and, perhaps, the action. For example, the line might read, "The *mouse stood* on the . . ." on the front side, *counter* on the back side. A 9x12 piece of construction paper would work well here. Students could be directed to fold it in half and to cut out a hole in the middle of the top half only. Next they could find a picture of an object in a magazine and paste it inside the folded paper. Then students write the start of the sentence on the front and the final word on the inside.

Cross-Curricular Activities

Language Arts: This story is circular in nature in that the cat ends up right where he started. To reinforce this type of story structure, give each of fifteen students a card or picture of where the cat sat. Have them stand in a circle in the same order as the cat sat in the book. Then use the book to check their sequence.

The Arts: This book also lends itself well to choral reading. Once students are in the circle noted above, have the whole class chant, "The cat sat on the . . ." and the child holding a given picture state the word. You might even want to put the chant to music!

Carle, Eric
Have You Seen My Cat?

Illustrated by the author
Scholastic, 1987. ISBN: 0-590-44461-1

Annotation

A boy is in search of his lost cat. He meets several people as he continues on his journey to find his cat. "Have you seen my cat?" he asks each of them. Each person points the boy in the direction of a cat that is not his. Not until the very end does the boy find *his* cat causing him to exclaim, "This is my cat!" Each cat is a different type that actually exists, making this an informational book of sorts.

Innovation

Ask students to list other items that could be lost (e.g., hat, coat, bird, dog). Suggest that each choose an object that could be lost and use this sentence frame to create a book similar to Carle's. See pages 12 and 13 for additional ideas for innovating on text.

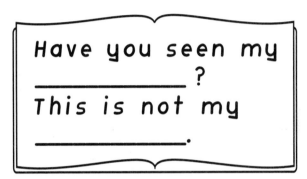

Have you seen my
_____?
This is not my
_____.

Cross-Curricular Activities

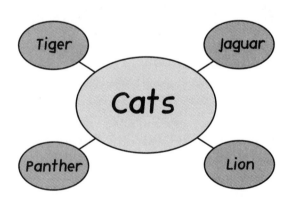

Language Arts: Have students name the types of cats shown in the book. As they do so, create a semantic map that shows the names. Create a map like the one at the left, using another animal such as dogs.

Social Studies: For a *geography* lesson, use a large map to show children where each cat in the book actually lives in its natural habitat. Place the name of the cat or a picture of it in the correct location on the map.

Curtis, Jamie Lee

When I Was Little: A Four-Year-Old's Memoir of Her Youth

Illustrated by Laura Cornell
HarperCollins, 1993. ISBN: 0-06-021079-6

Annotation

A four-year-old girl tells anecdotes about herself when she was little. She contrasts each statement with what she is able to do now that she is older and wiser!

Innovation

Discuss with students things that they can do now that they couldn't do when they were younger. You might want to list these on a chart or board. Suggest that students create their own book of memoirs using this basic pattern. Additional ways for innovating are on pages 12 and 13.

> When I was little,
> I_____.
> Now I
> _____.

Cross-Curricular Activities

The Arts: Have children create a time line for each year of their lives. A picture could represent a significant event for each year. This could be completed at home with parents and shared at school.

School	Playground	Home
I can read fast.	I can swing high.	I can reach the sink.
I can add.	I can climb.	

Social Studies: Ask each student to bring a clean can to school. Label each with a label that reads "I can." At the end of every day or week, ask students to think about something they can now do that they couldn't do at the start of the week. Then ask students to write each newly acquired skill on a slip of paper or a 3x5 index card and place the card(s) in their "I can" cans. These cards could also be used for a classification activity in which each student groups "can do's" into like categories. "Things I can do at school," "Things I can do at home," Things I can do on the playground" are some possible categories.

Additional *C*'s

Calmenson, Stephanie. *Dinner at the Panda Palace*. New York: Harper Collins, 1991.

—. *What Am I? Very First Riddles*. New York: Harper Trophy, 1989.

Campbell, Rod. *Dear Zoo*. New York: Puffin, 1982.

Cameron, Polly. *"I Can't" Said the Ant*. New York: Scholastic, 1961.

Capucilli, Alyssa. *Good Morning, Pond*. New York: Hyperion, 1994.

Carle, Eric. *Draw Me a Star*. New York: Scholastic, 1992.

—. *Pancakes, Pancakes*. New York: Scholastic, 1990.

—. *The Very Hungry Caterpillar*. New York: Scholastic, 1969.

Carlson, Nancy. *I Like Me*. New York: Puffin, 1988.

Carlstrom, Nancy. *Happy Birthday, Jesse Bear*. New York: Macmillan, 1994.

—. *Rise and Shine*. New York: Harper Collins, 1993.

—. *How Do You Say It Today, Jesse Bear?* New York: Macmillan, 1992.

—. *Better Not Get Wet, Jesse Bear*. New York: Macmillan, 1988.

Carter, David. *More Bugs in Boxes*. New York: Simon & Schuster.

Casey, Patricia. *My Cat Jack*. Cambridge, MA: Candlewick, 1994.

Cauley, Lorinda. *Treasure Hunt*. New York: G.P. Putnam's Sons, 1994.

—. *Clap Your Hands*. New York: Scholastic, 1992.

—. *The Animal Kids*. New York: Random House, 1979.

Causley, Charles. *"Quack" Said the Billy Goat*. New York: Harper & Row, 1986.

Cazet, Denys. *Nothing At All*. New York: Orchard, 1994.

Chandra, Deborah. *Miss Mabel's Table*. New York: Browndeer/Harcourt Brace, 1994.

Chapman, Cheryl. *Pass the Fritters, Critters*. New York: Four Winds Press, 1993.

Charlip, Remy. *Fortunately*. New York: Four Winds Press, 1987.

—. *What Good Luck! What Bad Luck!* New York: Scholastic, 1969.

Chase, Edith Newlin & Barbara Reid. *The New Baby Calf*. New York: Scholastic, 1984.

Cherry, Lynne. *Who's Sick Today?*. New York: Puffin/Unicorn, 1988.

Christlelow, Eileen. *Five Little Monkeys Sitting in a Tree*. New York: Clarion, 1991.

Coerr, Eleanor. *Chang's Paper Pony*. New York: Harper & Row, 1986.

Cohen, Caron Lee. *Three Yellow Dogs*. New York: Greenwillow, 1980.

Cole, Brock. *The King at the Door*. New York: Doubleday, 1979.

Collins, Pat. *I Am an Artist*. Brookfield, CT: Millbrook, 1992.

Conover, Chris. *Six Little Ducks*. New York: Crowell, 1976.

Cook, Bernadine. *The Little Fish That Got Away*. Addison-Wesley, 1976.

Cooke, Trish. *So Much*. Cambridge, MA: Candlewick, 1994.

Craft, Ruth & Erik Blegrad. *The Winter Bear*. New York: Macmillan, 1979.

Crews, Donald. *Freight Train*. New York: Scholastic, 1978.

—. *Ten Black Dots*. New York: Scholastic, 1968.

—. *We Read: A to Z*. New York: Greenwillow, 1967.

Cummings, Pat. *Clean Your Room, Harvey Moon!*. New York: Aladdin, 1994.

Curran, Eileen. *Life in the Sea*. Mahwah, NJ: Troll, 1985.

Cushman, Doug. *The ABC Mystery*. New York: Harper Collins, 1993.

Cutts, David. *The House That Jack Built*. Mahwah, NJ: Troll, 1979.

Cuyler, Margery. *That's Good! That's Bad!* New York: Henry Holt, 1991.

Dodd, Anne Wescott

Footprints and Shadows

Illustrated by Henri Sorensen
Simon and Schuster, 1992. ISBN: 0-671-78716-0

Annotation

This book addresses two fascinations of childhood – footprints and shadows. There are several examples of footprints and what causes them to go away. Half way through the book, the question shifts to shadows. Again, shadows are provided for different objects along with reasons for the shadows' disappearance.

Innovation

Invite students to tell about the kind of footprints they have made and what caused them to disappear. Using the suggestions stated on pages 12 and 13 to create an additional book. The book could be about students, footprints and shadows, or another noun could be substituted to create a book about another topic.

where do
_____ go?

Cross-Curricular Activities

The Arts: Provide students with a mound of soft clay and have them make their handprint in it. Ask them if they think their handprint will stay or disappear like those stated in the book. What would cause it to stay? What would cause it to disappear?

As an art activity, have students use tempera paint to make prints of various objects.

Science: Provide students with the opportunity to learn more about shadows. Take them out on the playground on a sunny day and ask them questions such as the following: Do they have a shadow? Why? Where is their shadow — in front or in back? Why? Does their shadow change in size? What would cause a shadow to disappear? Does every object have a shadow?

Dragonwagon, Crescent

Alligator Arrived with Apples: A Potluck Alphabet Feast

Illustrated by Jose Aruego and Arianee Dewey
Aladdin/Macmillan, 1992. ISBN: 0-689-71613-3

Annotation

Several animals decide to celebrate Thanksgiving together. The challenge? Each animal must bring a food that begins with the same letter of the animal's name. Each letter of the alphabet is represented by both animal and food in this friendly feast.

Innovation

Review the animals and foods that were brought to the feast. You might want to write each next to the letter of the alphabet that they represent. Suggest that children's names be substituted for the animals' names to create a similar book. Keep the beginning and ending the same. The suggestions on pages 12 and 13 might be of additional help.

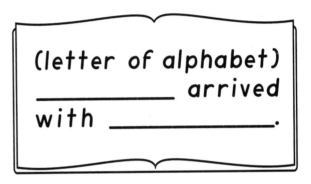

(letter of alphabet)
_____ arrived
with _____.

Cross-Curricular Activities

Language Arts: Provide each child with a page that shows one animal and the food associated with it in the book. Ask children to stand in alphabetical order. Then invite the whole class to chant the opening of the book which you have written on a chart large enough for all to see. Children, in turn, solo read the animal and food they are holding. At the very end, have the whole group chant the last two pages of the book, again written on a chart large enough for all to see.

Science/Health: Provide groups of children with cards showing the foods mentioned in the book. Ask them to categorize the foods into the various food groups. This activity could be extended by having children plan three balanced meals. Pictures from the various categories could be placed on three different paper plates to show three balanced meals according to the food pyramid.

Dunbar, Joyce
Seven Sillies

Illustrated by Chris Dunbar
Artists & Writers Guild Book (Golden Books), 1993. ISBN: 0-307-17504-9

Annotation

Without realizing it, several animals see their reflections in a pond. They decide that they need to capture these sillies by jumping in after them. They soon discover that they were seeing their reflections. Perhaps the silliest of all, however, is frog who told them they needed to jump in the first place. After all, it's frog who can't count!

Innovation

Review the order of the animals as they came to look in the pond. Use the frame shown at the right and the suggestions on pages 12 and 13 to have students create another book.

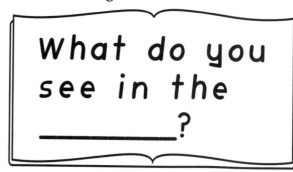

what do you see in the _____?

Cross-Curricular Activities

Science: This book lends itself to learning about reflections. Ask children to look in a mirror. What do they see? Ask them to suggest other places they might see their reflections (e.g., car, window, lake).

beautiful sheep

handsome pig

Language Arts: Write each adjective used to describe each animal and the animal's name on two separate cards. Place the cards in the pocket holder in mixed order. Have students place the adjective next to the animal so that their response matches the book. Once finished, take another look at the book to check. Then ask students for additional words that could be used to describe the animals. Write these words on cards and place them in the appropriate place in the pocket holder. Have students read the descriptions for each animal. Students could then use these cards independently during their free time.

Additional *D*'s

Dahl, Roald. *Dirty Beasts*. New York: Farrar, Strauss & Giroux, 1983.

Dayton, Laura. *LeRoy's Birthday Circus*. Nelson, 1981.

Degen, Bruce. *Teddy Bear Towers*. New York: HarperCollins, 1991.

——. *Jamberry*. New York: HarperCollins, 1983.

Delany, A. *The Butterfly*. New York: Crown, 1977.

Demarest, Chris. *No Peas for Nellie*. New York: Aladdin, 1988.

Demers, Jan. *What Do You Do With a . . .?* Pinellas, FL: Willowisp, 1985.

Demi. *Demi's Count the Animals 1-2-3*. New York: Grossett, 1986.

Deming, Alhambra. *Who Is Tapping at My WIndow?* New York: Puffin, 1988.

DeRegniers, Beatrice. *So Many Cats!* New York; Clarion, 1985.

——. *It Does Not Say Meow*. New York: Clarion, 1972.

——. *May I Bring a Friend?* New York: Atheneum, 1972.

——. *What Can You Do with a Shoe?* New York: Harper & Row, 1955.

Dodd, Lynley. *Hairy Maclary Scattercat*. Gareth Stevens, 1988.

——. *Hairy Maclary's Bone*. Gareth Stevens, 1985.

——. *Hairy Maclary from Donaldson's Dairy*. Gareth Stevens, 1985.

——. *The Nickle Nackle Tree*. New York: Macmillan, 1976.

Dodds, Dayle Ann. *Do Bunnies Talk?* New York: HarperCollins, 1992.

——. *Wheel Away*. New York: Harper Trophy, 1989.

Domanska, Janina. *If All the Seas Were One Sea*. New York: Macmillan, 1987.

——. *Busy Monday Morning*. New York: Greenwillow, 1985.

——. *What Do You See?* New York: Greenwillow, 1974.

——. *The Turnip*. New York: Macmillan, 1969.

Donnelly, Liza. *Dinosaur Garden*. New York: Scholastic, 1995.

Dragonwagon, Crescent. *The Itch Book*. New York: Macmillan, 1990.

——. *This Is the Bread I Baked for Ned*. New York: Macmillan, 1989.

——. *Half a Moon and One Whale Star*. New York: Macmillan, 1986.

Driz, Dusei. *The Boy and the Tree*. New York: Prentice-Hall, 1978.

Dubanevich, Arlene. *Tom's Trail*. New York: Viking, 1990.

Duke, Kate. *Seven Froggies Went to School*. New York: Dutton, 1985.

Duncan, Lois. *Birthday Mood*. New York: Viking, 1989.

Dunrea, Olivier. *Deep Down Underground*. New York: Aladdin, 1993.

——. *Mogwogs on the March!* New York: Holiday House, 1985.

Ekker, Ernst

What Is Beyond the Hill?

Illustrated by Hilde Heyduck-Huth
Lippincott, 1985. ISBN: 0-397-32166-X

Annotation

Two children ask questions to discover what is beyond the hill and the world. As each question is answered, they increase their awareness of their world and of the universe. The succeeding pictures in the book show the previous pictures, illustrating how the small parts contribute to the larger picture.

Innovation

Use the suggestions on pages 12 and 13 and the frame below to have children create their own books.

What's beyond ____ ?
Is the end
of the world there?

Cross-Curricular Activities

The Arts: Help children better understand perspective, or how things can look smaller or larger in a picture. Cut two "mountains" out of construction paper, one darker and larger than the other. Draw details, like snowcaps, with white crayon. Paste the lighter and smaller mountain above and to the side of the larger mountain on a piece of background paper. Invite students to discuss which mountain looks closer, and why. Encourage them to repeat this activity with other shapes they choose.

Science: Talk about what composes the earth. Bring in a model of the earth showing the layers of the earth. Then give students a large circle to label with the layers of the earth. Each layer could be colored a different color.

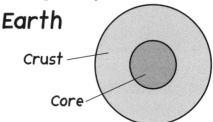

Earth

Crust

Core

Ets, Marie

Elephant in a Well

Illustrated by the author
Viking Press, 1972. ISBN: 670-29169-2

Annotation

A young elephant falls into a well and can't get out. In turn, several animals come by and try to pull out the elephant but can't. Then mouse comes along. Although the other animals laugh at the thought of mouse being able to help, it is his strength that gives enough extra energy to enable all of them to pull elephant out of the well.

Innovation

Use the frame shown below and suggestions on pages 12 and 13 to encourage children to write a book similar to this one.

_____ fell into a _____ and couldn't get out. _____ came along and wanted to help. Alone, _____ couldn't pull _____ out of the _____.

Cross-Curricular Activities

The Arts: After having student's recall the animals in the story, suggest that they retell it, acting it out as they go. Use chairs to create a circle to function as the well. Write each animal's name on a paper plate and attach a piece of yarn to the paper plate, long enough so that it can be draped over a students head. Next pass out the paper plates to students. Ask one or two students who weren't assigned a part to retell the story. As the animals appear in the story, have children gather around the well and reenact trying to pull elephant out of the well.

Language Arts: You might want to tell students that some stories have a moral, or lesson. Then invite them to state whether or not they think this story has a moral. What do they think it is? Why do they think so?

Social Studies: This book lends itself to discussing how important team work can be. Ask students to think of things that are easier to do because of the help of others. Students could also share ways they help a group to complete a given task.

Evans, Katie

Hunky Dory Ate It

Illustrated by Janet Morgan Stoeke
Dutton, 1992. ISBN: 0-525-44847-0

Annotation

Hunky Dory is a dog who likes to eat just about everything. In this story he eats so many different things that he gets sick. His owner takes Hunky to the vet who gives him something else to eat – medicine. Hunky eats it, but the pictures make it clear that this is one item he doesn't like.

Innovation

Have students use the basic pattern and their own names to create a page for a class book.

Michael Rooky
made a cookie.

Cross-Curricular Activities

Langage Arts: After students have had the opportunity to make a rhyme associated with their names, ask them to sit in a circle. In turn, students read their page with the whole class chiming in with "Hunky Dory ate it!" after each page is shared. This book lends itself well to reviewing rhyming words. Write each pair of rhyming words on cards. Distribute them to the students and have them play match up by allowing them to move around the room until they find their partner. Once found, have them stand or sit by their partner. The pair could then write a rhyme using both words.

Science/Health: You might want to have students talk about their diets. What makes them function well? poorly? This could lead into discussing the food pyramid and recommended daily allowances.

Additional *E*'s

Eastman, Patricia. *Sometimes Things Change.* Chicago: Children's Press, 1983.

—. *Are You My Mother?* New York: Random House, 1960.

Eastwick, Ivy. *Rainbow Over All.* McKay, 1970.

Eberts, Marjorie & Margaret Gisler. *Pancakes, Crackers, & Pizza.* Chicago: Children's Press, 1984.

Edelman, Elaine. *Boom-de-Boom.* Pantheon, 1980.

Edwards, Dorothy & Jenny Williams. *A Wet Monday.* New York: Morrow, 1976.

Ehlert, Lois. *Nuts to You.* New York: Harcourt Brace, 1993.

—. *Feathers for Lunch.* New York: Harcourt Brace, 1990.

—. *Eating the Alphabet.* San Diego: Harcourt Brace, 1989.

Ehrlich, Amy. *Parents in the Pigpen, Pigs in the Tub.* New York: Dial, 1994.

—. *Leo, Zack, & Emmie.* New York: Dial, 1981.

Eichenberg, Fritz. *Ape in a Cape.* New York: Harcourt Brace, 1973.

Einsel, Walter. *Did You Ever See?* New York: Scholastic, 1962.

Egan, Louise. *The Farmer in the Dell.* New York: Whitman, 1987.

Elkin, Benjamin. *The King Who Could Not Sleep.* New York: Parents, 1975.

—. *Such Is the Way of the World.* New York: Parents, 1968.

—. *Why the Sun Was Late.* New York: Parents, 1966.

—. *Six Foolish Fisherman.* New York: Scholastic, 1957.

Elliott, David. *An Alphabet of Rotten Kids!* New York: Philomel, 1992.

Elting, Mary and Michael Folson. *Q is for Duck.* New York: Clarion, 1980.

Emberly, Barbara. *One Wide River to Cross.* Englewood Cliffs, NJ: Prentice-Hall, 1966.

—. *Simon's Song.* Englewood Cliffs, NJ: Prentice-Hall, 1969.

—. *Night's Nice.* New York: Doubleday, 1963.

Emberly, Ed. *Go Away, Big Green Monster!* New York: Little Brown, 1992.

—. Klippity Klop. Boston: Little Brown, 1974.

Enderle, Judith & Stephanie Tessler. *Six Creepy Sheep.* New York: Penguin Group, 1992.

Esbensen, Barbara. *Who Shrank My Grandmother's House?* New York: HarperCollins, 1992.

Esterl, Arnica. *The Fine Round Cake.* New York: Four Winds Press, 1991.

Ets, Marie Hall. *Just Me.* New York: Viking, 1965.

—. *Play with Me.* New York: Viking, 1955.

Eurremer, Teryl. *After Dark.* New York: Crown, 1989.

Evans, Eva. *Sleepy Time.* Boston: Houghton Mifflin, 1962.

Evans, Mel. *The Tiniest Sound.* New York: Doubleday, 1969.

Falwell, Cathryn
Feast for 10

Illustrated by the author
Scholastic, 1993. ISBN: 0-590-48466-4

Annotation

A family goes to the grocery store to buy the ingredients for a feast that will feed ten. All family members help in the shopping, unloading, preparing, and consuming. This is an excellent book for showing the benefits of group work.

Innovation

Let children talk about foods they enjoy and some of the feasts they have had in their homes. Suggest that they create their own number books using the numbers 1–10 just like Falwell. You may also want to use some of the suggestions listed on pages 12 and 13.

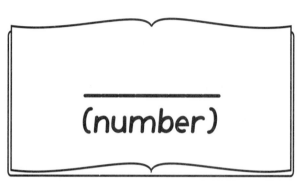

Cross-Curricular Activities

Mathematics: If you purchase any goods that have labels, save them to use as illustrations for the creation of a class book entitled "Our Feast for 28." Under each label, have students state the number and the type of container used for each, for example, "twenty green beans in a can."

Science/Health: You might want to use this book to help students further understand food groups. Plan a balanced meal with students making a list of all necessary ingredients. Next, take students to the grocery store where each can do a part of the shopping. Once back at school, have students prepare the lunch or dinner for all to share. This activity could lead to several additional activities such as estimating, reading recipes, and fractions.

Social Studies: This book could be used to talk about how family members contribute to one another. Ask children to name ways that they help out and make a list for all to see. Perhaps they will take away new ways they might help out at home.

Fleming, Denise

Barnyard Banter

Illustrated by the author
Henry Holt, 1994. ISBN: 0-8050-1957-X

Annotation

Animals make sounds as this book shows. Each farm animal is shown along with the sound it makes. Also shown is where the farm animal is kept while living on the farm.

Innovation

After having children review the animals and their sounds, suggest that they use the same format to create a book about another group of animals, such as zoo animals.

_____ in the _____,

_____
_____ (record sounds on
_____ these three lines)

Cross-Curricular Activities

Language Arts: Use this book to help students further understand intonation. Have them look at the way the word *honk* is written and ask them why they think the author wrote it this way. Suggest that the author wanted the reader to read with different volumes, and model how this can

Animal	Sound	Habitat
Bear	Growl	Forrest
Lion		
Coyote		

be done. Then have children do so. They might want to use the same technique in the creation of their own books.

Science/Mathematics: On separate cards, write each animal, the sound it makes, and the place where it lives. Have students group the three together in a pocket chart that shows the three categories: Animal, Sound, Habitat.

Fox, Mem

Time for Bed

Illustrated by Jane Dyer
Gulliver/Harcourt Brace, 1993. ISBN: 0-15-288183-2

Annotation

Parent animals and their babies are shown in this book. Each parent prepares the baby for sleep with the use of a rhyme that also uses repetition.

Innovation

Reverse the sequence and invite children to create an awakening story. Each of the animals in the book could be used, or students could suggest other animals. Students might also like to think of other pairs of parent/baby animals and use the same format as Fox to create a similar book.

> It's time to awaken,
> little _____, little _____.
> Daylight is showing over all the _____.
> It's time for _____,
> little _____, little _____.

Cross-Curricular Activities

Language Arts: Write each pair of rhyming words on a sentence strip and read them with the students. Then cut apart each pair, mix them up, and have students find and match the pairs. You could also do some initial consonant substitution by making "flip" cards. Write one of the words on a card. Then, on a card that will cover only the first letter, write a letter that will make a new word, the same one used in the book, when placed on top of the word card. Tape this to the first card. Have students "flip" as they practice reading the words.

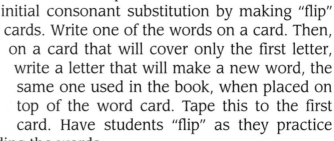

Science: Provide students with names that are used for adult and baby animals. Have them locate each in the book.

Additional *F*'s

Farber, Norma. *How to Ride a Tiger*. Boston: Houghton Mifflin, 1983.

——. *Never Say Ugh to a Bug*. New York: Greenwillow, 1979.

——. *Small Wonders. Coward*, 1979.

——. *There Goes Featherstop!* New York: Unicorn-Dutton, 1979.

——. *Up the Down Elevator*. New York: Addison-Wesley, 1979.

——. *There Was a Woman Who Married a Man*. New York: Addison-Wesley, 1978.

——. *Where's Gomer?* New York: Dutton, 1974.

——. *As I Was Crossing Boston Common*. New York: Dutton, 1973.

Farjeon, Eleanor. *Cats Sleep Anywhere*. New York: Lippincott, 1990.

Fehlner, Paul. *Dog and Cat*. Chicago: Children's Press, 1990.

Fenton, Edward. *The Big Yellow Balloon*. New York: Doubleday, 1967.

Field, Rachel. *A Road Might Lead to Anywhere*. New York: Lippincott, 1990.

——. *General Store*. New York: Greenwillow, 1988.

Fisher, Aileen. *When It Comes to Bugs*. New York: Harper, 1986.

Fisher, Leonard. *Boxes! Boxes! Boxes!* New York: Viking, 1984.

Flack, Marjorie. *Ask Mr. Bear*. New York: Macmillan, 1932.

Fleming, Denise. *In the Tall, Tall Grass*. New York: Holt, 1992.

——. *Lunch*. New York: Holt, 1992.

Flora, James. *The Day the Cow Sneezed*. New York: Harcourt Brace, 1957.

Foster, Joanna. *Pete's Puddle*. New York: Harcourt Brace, 1950.

Foulds, Eldrida Vipont. *The Elephant and the Bad Baby*. Coward, 1986.

Fowler, Susi Gregg. *When Summer Ends*. New York: Greenwillow, 1989.

Fox, Mem. *Tough Boris*. New York: Harcourt Brace, 1994.

——. *Shoes from Grandpa*. New York: Orchard, 1989.

——. *Arabella the Smallest Girl in the World*. New York: Scholastic, 1987.

——. *Hattie and the Fox*. New York: Bradbury Press, 1986.

Freschet, Berniece. *The Ants Go Marching*. New York: Scribner's, 1973.

Funakoshi, Canna. *One Evening*. Saxonville, MA: Picture Book Studio, 1988.

——. *One Morning*. Saxonville, MA: Picture Book Studio, 1986.

Fyleman, Rose. *A Fairy Went a Marketing*. New York: Puffin/Unicorn, 1986.

Gackenbach, Dick

Supposes

Illustrated by the author
Harcourt Brace, 1989. ISBN: 0-15-200594-3

Annotation

Did you know that a cat who eats lemons is a sourpuss? Did you know that stubbing his toe makes a dino-sore? Playing with words to create new words is what this book is all about.

Innovation

Suggest that children create their own supposes about an animal or object of choice. You might want to use one or more of the suggestions on pages 12 and 13.

Suppose _____.

Cross-Curricular Activities

The Arts: Have students work in pairs to create different animals. Give each a piece of paper and ask one person to draw the top half of the body, the other to create the bottom half. They could do this without looking at the other half and then try to put them together. Once assembled, have students create a name for their animal.

Language Arts: You might also want to do a brief lesson on word etymology. Show students where different words, such as *sandwich,* originated. Ask them to think of other words they use and guess how they might have come to be.

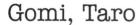

Gomi, Taro

Who Hid It?

Illustrated by the author
Millbrook Press, 1991. ISBN: 1-56294-011-2

Annotation

Different objects are hidden in different animals. A question such as "Who hid the glove?" is posed along with its picture on the left-hand page. On the facing page, two like animals are shown, one of which is hiding the object mentioned and shown on the previous page.

Innovation

Provide children with the sentence pattern used throughout the book and allow them to create their own books of hidden objects. You might also want to have the students change the verb, providing them with the following pattern:

> Who hid the _____?
> Who _____ the _____?

Cross-Curricular Activities

Science: Make a list of animals that use camouflage to avoid danger. Have students construct habitats for given animals. Point out how habitat can often function as a form of camouflage.

Language Arts: Generate several action words that could be used in place of *hid*. Write each of these on a card. Do the same for nouns. Place the sentence frame, "Who _____the_____?" in a pocket chart. Have students place different action words in the first space, nouns in the second, and read the newly constructed question.

Guarino, Deborah

Is Your Mama a Llama?

Illustrated by Steven Kellogg
Scholastic, 1989. ISBN:0-590-44725-4

Annotation

A young llama goes looking for his mother and asks the same question of each animal he meets, "Is your mama a llama?" Each animal says no and then proceeds to describe its mother – what she looks like, where she lives, and/or what sounds she makes – in rhyme. Finally, he asks his friend who helps the llama discover his mother!

Innovation

Use one or more suggestions provided on pages 12 and 13 and the basic question shown below to have students learn about other animals.

Is your mama a _____?

Cross-Curricular Activities

Language Arts: Allow students to select a given animal and ask them to find out three facts about it — what it looks like, where it lives, and any additional fact that they find interesting. In turn, invite each to lead the class through a guessing game through the use of the facts. For example, the child could say, "My animal lives in the water and its babies hatch from eggs. What is it?"

Science/Mathematics: Have students take a look through the book and note the animals that are included. As they name each, write them on cards. Next, have students group the animals with like characteristics (e.g. birds, mammals). Ask them if there are other groups that aren't included.

Social Studies: Using a large world map, show students where each animal lives in its natural habitat.

Additional *G*'s

Gackenbach, Dick. *A Bag Full of Pups*. Boston: Houghton Mifflin, 1981.

Gag, Wanda. *Millions of Cats*. New York: Scholastic, 1956.

Gage, Wilson. *Squash Pie*. New York: Greenwillow, 1976.

Galdone, Paul. *The Little Red Hen*. Boston: Houghton Mifflin, 1985.

Galloway, Priscilla. *When You Were Little and I Was Big*. Toronto: Annick, 1984.

Garelick, May. *Where Does the Butterfly Go When It Rains?* New York: Scholastic, 1961.

Gelman, Rita. *Cats and Mice*. New York: Scholastic, 1985.

——. *The Biggest Sandwich Ever*. New York: Scholastic, 1980.

——. *More Spaghetti I Say*. New York: Scholastic, 1977.

——. *Hello, Cat You Need a Hat*. New York: Scholastic, 1979.

Gerstein, Mordicai. *William, Where Are You?* New York: Crown, 1985.

——. *Roll Over!* New York: Crown, 1984.

Gibbons, Gail. *The Seasons of Arnold's Apple* Tree. New York: Harcourt Brace, 1984.

Gilman, Phoebe. *Something from Nothing*. New York: Scholastic, 1992.

——. *Jillian Jiggs*. New York: Scholastic, 1985.

Ginsburg, Mirra. *Asleep, Asleep*. New York: Greenwillow, 1992.

——. *Across the Stream*. Mulberry, 1982.

——. *Good Morning, Chick*. New York: Greenwillow, 1980.

——. *The Sun's Asleep Behind the Hill*. New York: Greenwillow, 1982.

——. *The Strongest One of All*. New York: Greenwillow, 1977.

——. *The Chick and the Duckling*. New York: Macmillan, 1972.

Goennel, Heidi. *My Day*. Boston: Little Brown, 1988.

Gomi, Taro. *Bus Stops*. San Francisco: Chronicle, 1988.

——. *Who Ate It?* Brookfield, CT: Millbrook, 1988.

——. *Coco Can't Wait!* New York: Morrow, 1984.

Gordon, Sharon. *Drip Drop*. Mahwah, NJ: Troll, 1981.

Goss, Janet & Jerome Harste. *It Didn't Frighten Me!* New York: Scholastic, 1988.

Graboff, Abner (illustrator). *Old MacDonald Had a Farm*. New York: Scholastic, 1969.

Graham, Bob. *Here Comes Theo*. Boston: Little Brown, 1983.

Graham, John. *I Love You, Mouse*. New York: Harcourt Brace, 1976.

——. *A Crowd of Cows*. New York: Scholastic, 1968.

Greeley, Valerie. *The Acorn's Story*. New York: Macmillan, 1994.

——. *White Is the Moon*. New York: Macmillan, 1990.

——. *Where's My share?* New York: Macmillan, 1989.

Greenberg, David. *Slugs*. Boston: Little Brown, 1983.

Greenberg, Polly. *Oh Lord, I Wish I Was a Buzzard*. New York: Macmillan, 1968.

Greene, Carol. *The Insignificant Elephant*. New York: Harcourt Brace, 1985.

Griffith, Helen, V. *Alex and the Cat*. New York: Greenwillow, 1982.

——. *Mine Will, Said John*. New York: Greenwillow, 1980.

Grossman, Bill. *Donna O'Neeshuck Was Chased by Some Cows*. New York: Harper Trophy, 1988.

Grossman, Virginia. *Seven Little Rabbits*. San Francisco: Chronicle, 1991.

Grover, Max. *The Accidental Zucchini: An Unexpected Alphabet*. Harcourt Brace, 1993.

Gwynne, Fred. *Easy to See Why*. New York: Simon & Schuster, 1994.

Halsey, Megan
Jump for Joy: A Book of Months

Illustrated by the author
Bradbury Press, 1994. ISBN: 0-02-742040-X

Annotation

This book highlights each month of the year through the use of alliteration. "Jumping for joy in January," "juggling jacks in June," and "admiring artists in August" are examples that show how the months are tied in with alliteration.

Innovation

Ask students to name things they like to do in each month. Then suggest that they create their own book of months beginning most words with the same letter that starts the name of the month. You might want to have them use the frame shown here. The innovation suggestions on pages 12 and 13 provide some additional ideas for ways to publish student innovations.

Cross-Curricular Activities

The Arts: Have children create a calendar for the classroom. This could be completed in pairs or in small groups. Write the name of each month on a slip of paper and place each into a paper bag. Divide the class into pairs or groups and have one person from each draw out one card. Ask the group to think of significant events that happen in the month they've selected. Then, on a large piece of paper, have them create a collage that depicts these events. Also provide each group with another large piece of paper which has been divided into enough spaces to fill in the days for the month. Have them attach their illustration and day sections together, creating a page for the class calendar. Sequence these, placing the current month on a calendar bulletin board. Use the calendar for daily calendar activities.

Mathematics: Use this book to help students learn about the 12 months. First, draw a large circle on the board or on a chart. Write the word *year* in the center of the circle. Next, divide the circle into twelve sections, one for each month of the year. Now have students recall the months they remember, writing them in the correct order around the circle. Then, if necessary, fill in the missing spaces on the wheel. As you are writing the months, point out that the first letter of each month is capitalized. Also point out that 12 months make one year and that the months appear in a certain order. Refer students back to the book as you check to see if each month is listed in order on the wheel.

Harshman, Marc

Only One

Illustrated by Barbara Garrison
Cobblehill Books, 1993. ISBN: 0-525-65116-0

Annotation

Many parts create a whole as this book well illustrates. Set at a county fair, several examples such as 500 seeds in one pumpkin, 10 cents in one dime, 8 horses on one merry-go-round, and 4 wheels on one wagon are provided.

Innovation

Ask students to take a look around the classroom and look for objects that show part-to-whole relationships. They might discover, for example, that there are several coats but only one closet, several paints but only one art center, and so on. Next, suggest that they create a book about these relationships. You might want to have students work in pairs to complete this activity. The frame shown here might be of help as might the suggestions shown on pages 12 and 13.

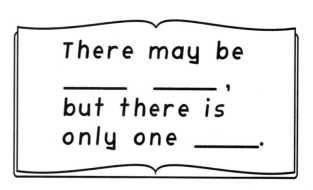

There may be
_____ _____,
but there is
only one _____.

Cross-Curricular Activities

Language Arts: Brainstorm a list of things that could be seen at a county fair. Have students compare their list with the items mentioned in the book.

Mathematics: Bring in several sizes of squash or pumpkins and have students estimate how many seeds they think are in each. These estimations could be written on different slips of paper and put into an estimation jar. Then cut open each squash or pumpkin and have students count the seeds. How close were they? Did size have anything to do with the number of seeds?

Social Studies: If you use this book at the beginning of the year, you might want to put each child's name or picture on a puzzle piece and have the class assemble the puzzle. The heading? There may be many individuals but there is only one great class!

Hutchins, Pat
My Best Friend

Illustrated by the author
Greenwillow, 1993. ISBN: 0-688-11485-7

Annotation

Being a friend means liking and appreciating a person for who they are. Two little girls remind us of this as they talk about what they can do and what their friends can do. Although each has different abilities, they're still best friends.

Innovation

After talking with the children about the friendship that the two girls share, ask them to talk about their friends. What specific things can their friends do? What can they do that their friend can't? Suggest that they use the frame shown here to create their own books about a very best friend. The innovation suggestions listed on pages 12 and 13 might also be of help.

My best friend
can _____.
I can _____.

Cross-Curricular Activities

Language Arts: Have children make a "friendship" acrostic. This activity could be completed by pairs, small groups, or with the entire class. Ask them to write one quality for each letter of the word *friendship*.

Social Studies: Ask children to tell what friendship means to them. Perhaps you could create a semantic map that shows the word *friendship* in the center and their suggestions branching out from it.

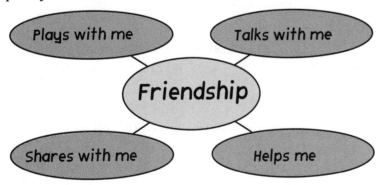

Plays with me · Talks with me · Friendship · Shares with me · Helps me

Additional *H*'s

Hague, Kathleen. *Alphabears*. New York: Scholastic, 1984.

Haas, Jessie. *Busybody Brandy*. New York: Greenwillow, 1994.

Hall, Donald. *I Am the Dog, I Am the Cat*. New York: Dial, 1994.

Hallinar, P. K. *We're Very Good Friends, My Sister and I*. Nashville, TN: Ideals Children's Books, 1989.

Hamm, Diane. *Rockabye Farm*. New York: Half Moon/Simon Schuster, 1992.

Hamsa, Bobbie. *Animal Babies*. Chicago: Children's Press, 1983.

Hansard, Peter. *Wag, Wag, Wag*. Cambridge, MA: Candlewick, 1993.

Hawkins, Colin & Jacqui Hawkins. *Old Mother Hubbard*. New York: Putnam's Sons, 1985.

Hayes, Sarah. *The Grumpalump*. New York: Clarion, 1990.

——. *This Is the Bear*. Cambridge, MA: Candlewick, 1986.

Heide, Florence P. & Roxanne Heide. *A Monster Is Coming! A Monster Is Coming!* New York: Franklin Watts, 1980.

Heide, Florence P. & Sylvia Worth Van Clief. *That's What Friends Are For*. New York: Four Winds Press, 1970.

Heilbroner, Joan. *This Is the House Where Jack Lives*. New York: Harper & Row, 1962.

Hellen, Nancy. *Old MacDonald Had a Farm*. New York: Orchard, 1990.

——. *The Bus Stop*. New York: Orchard.

Hennessy, B.G. *Jake Baked the Cake*. New York: Viking, 1990.

——. *School Days*. New York: Puffin, 1990.

Higgins, Don. *Papa's Going to Buy Me a Mockingbird*. New York: Seabury, 1968.

Hill, Eric. *Spot goes to School*. New York: Putnam's Sons, 1984.

——. *Where's Spot?* New York: Putnam, 1980.

Hindley, Judy. *Into the Jungle*. Cambridge, MA: Candlewick, 1994.

Hines, Anna. *Come to the Meadow*. New York: Clarion, 1984.

Hirsh, Marilyn. *Could Anything Be Worse?* New York: Holiday House, 1974.

Hoban,Lillian. *Arthur's Prize Reader*. New York: Harper & Row, 1978.

Hoberman, Mary Ann. *A House Is a House for Me*. New York: Scholastic, 1978.

Hoffman, Hilde. *The Green Grass Grows All Around*. New York: Macmillan, 1968.

Hogrogian, Nonny. *One Fine Day*. New York: Macmillan, 1971.

Hoguet, Susan R. *I Unpacked My Grandmother's Trunk*. New York: Dutton, 1983.

Hood, Thomas. *Before I Go to Sleep*. New York: G. P. Putnam's Sons, 1990.

Houston, John. *A Mouse in My House*. Reading, MA: Addison-Wesley, 1972.

Hudson, Cheryl & Bernette Ford. *Bright Eyes, Brown Skin*. New York: Scholastic, 1992.

Hughes, Shirley. *Chatting*. Cambridge, MA: Candlewick, 1994.

——. *Hiding*. Cambridge, MA: Candlewick, 1994.

——. *When We Went to the Park*. New York: Lothrop, Lee, & Shepard, 1985.

Hutchins, Pat. *Rosie's Walk*. New York: Scholastic, 1987.

——. *The Doorbell Rang*. New York: Mulberry, 1986.

——. *Don't Forget the Bacon*. New York: Greenwillow, 1976.

——. *The Wind Blew*. New York: Macmillan, 1974.

Hutchinson, Veronica S. *Henny Penny*. Boston: Little Brown, 1976.

Inkpen, Mick

Billy's Beetle

Illustrated by the author
Harcourt Brace, 1991. ISBN: 0-15-200427-0

Annotation

A boy loses his pet beetle and begins his search to find it. He is assisted by others as he searches, but it's the hedgehog, who is the last to join the search, who locates the beetle.

Innovation

Children might want to talk about things they have misplaced and tell how they found them. Next tell them that you have lost something in the room and that you need each person, in turn, to help you find it. As students join the search, give each the following page to fill in and illustrate.

I've lost my _____.
Help me find it!
Along came _____.

Students might like to create their own "lost" books using the form shown above. Also see pages 12 and 13 for additional publishing ideas.

Cross-Curricular Activities

The Arts: Have students use drama to remember this story. Choose one person to be the beetle. Have all students in the class cover their eyes while the beetle hides. Then choose other students to be Billy and the other animals in the book who helped Billy to find his beetle. Each student could be given a name tag to wear. Start off by having Billy say, "I've lost my beetle. Help me find it!" The class members not assigned a part say in unison, "Along came _____." When the character's name is mentioned, that child takes a quick look to find beetle, then stands in front of the class. Proceed in like manner until the last child, hedgehog, tries to find beetle in the classroom. If found, the hedgehog gets to be the beetle for the next round! If not, beetle chooses another child to be the beetle for the next round.

Social Studies: Ask students to tell about a time when they helped another person find a lost object. How long did it take? Where did they look? Did they ever find it?

Isadora, Rachel

I See

Illustrated by the author
Greenwillow, 1985. ISBN: 0-688-04059-4

Annotation

A young child states the things she sees on a given day. She also states what can be done with the objects she sees. The story ends with her seeing her crib and saying, "Good night."

Innovation

Allow children to state things that they see on any given day. Then have them choose another sense and create their own books to go with that sense. The frame shown below might be of help as might the suggestions on pages 12 and 13.

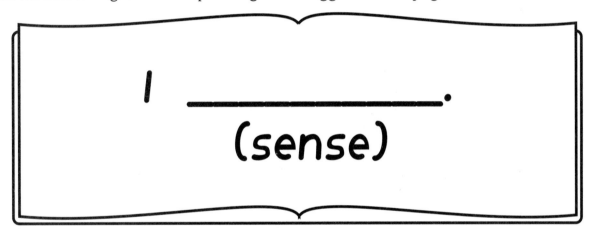

I _____.

(sense)

Cross-Curricular Activities

Science/Health: Use this book as a way to introduce more information about the eye. You might do this simple experiment to show them how the pupil works: Turn off the lights and have them look in small mirrors. Then, as you turn on the lights, have them note what happens to the pupil: Does it get larger? Smaller? Why?

Janovitz, Marilyn

Is It Time?

Illustrated by the author
North-South, 1994. ISBN: 1-55858-332-7

Annotation

A young wolf needs to go to bed. A series of questions takes the reader through the steps used to prepare for bed. Each succeeding page lists the new idea and repeats those already mentioned until, finally, the wolf climbs into bed and goes to sleep.

Innovation

Ask students to recall what happened first, second, and so on. Then have them talk about what they do as they get ready for bed. Suggest that they create a book to tell about how they prepare for bed, using the same repetitive pattern that Janovitz uses. The frame below might be of help as might the suggestions listed on pages 12 and 13.

Is it time to ___?
Yes, it's time to ___.

Cross-Curricular Activities

Language Arts: This book lends itself well to partner reading. One person could read the repeated line, "Yes it's time to _____." The other could read the question posed on each page. Both could read the cumulative lines when they appear.

The Arts: Teach students motions that could be used for the various actions mentioned in the book. Then, as you reread the book, have them act out the sentences using the actions.

Johnson, Richard

Look at Me in Funny Clothes!

Illustrated by Martin Chatterton
Candlewick, 1994. ISBN:1-56402-415-6

Annotation

Readers get the chance to see what they would look like if they wear different clothes. The book is shaped so that the readers can place the book around their necks. The picture below shows what they would look like if they were to take on a role such as skeleton, superhero and deep-sea diver.

Innovation

Ask students to name characters they would like to be. Suggest that they create their own books using the same format. Provide them with paper cut like the paper in the book. The frame below could also be used as could some of the suggestions listed on pages 12 and 13.

Cross-Curricular Activities

The Arts: You might want to bring in several items of clothing and allow children to dress up as certain characters. They could then tell about themselves as the given character.

Reading: Use the format shown above to have students report on the main character of a book or story they have read.

Social studies: Have students name community helpers or other occupations. Then have them design a page that shows the attire of a given helper or worker.

Jonas, Ann

Now We Can Go

Illustrated by the author
Greenwillow, 1986. ISBN: 0-688-04802-1

Annotation

A boy is going on a trip and wants to bring a few toys along. However, by the end of the book, the reader sees that the boy ends up placing all his toys from his toy box into the bag for his trip. Once the bag is loaded, he is ready to go.

Innovation

Ask students what they like to take with them when they go different places. Suggest that they write about what they would like to take. They might want to use a title similar to Jonas's.

Let's go!

Cross-Curricular Activities

Language Arts: Have students retell the story using the same objects that were mentioned in the book. Bring in a shopping bag and a cardboard box to function as the toy box.Place several objects in it. Have students, in turn, take one object from the toy box and put it into the shopping bag. Use the book to check whether or not students recalled the order of objects. You might want to assign a student to be the checker.

Mathematics: This book also lends itself well to addition and subtraction. Using the bag, objects and box as mentioned for the activity above, have students count the number of objects as you place them into the box. Next, choose one student to take one object from the box and place it into the bag. Ask, "If we had ten objects and took one away, how many do we have left?" Continue to the next object. This time, however, you can ask two questions. First ask, "If we had nine objects and took one away, how many do we have left?" Then ask, "If we had one toy in the bag and we added another, how many do we have in the bag?" Continue in like manner until all objects have been removed from the box and placed into the bag.

Additional *I*'s and *J*'s

Ipcar, Dahlov. *Hard Scrabble Harvest*. New York: Doubleday, 1976.

——. *The Cat Came Back*. New York: Knopf, 1971.

——. *Black and White*. New York: Knopf, 1963.

Isadora, Rachel. *I Hear*. New York: Greenwillow, 1985.

Ishinabe, Fusako. *Hiro's Pillow*. Ada, OK: Garrett, 1989.

Ivimey, John. *Three Blind Mice*. New York: Clarion, 1987.

Jabar. *Bored Blue? Think What You Can Do!* Boston: Little Brown, 1991.

Jacobs, Joseph. *Johnny-Cake*. New York: Viking, 1972.

——. *Master of All Masters*. New York: Grosset & Dunlap, 1972.

Jakob, Donna. *My Bike*. New York: Hyperion, 1994.

Jam, Teddy. *Night Cars*. New York: Watts, 1989.

James, Sara. *Boots Loses a Tooth*. New York: Smithmark, 1993.

James, Vincent. *My Favorite Monsters*. Standford, CT: Longmeadow, 1992.

Jarrell, Randell. *A Bat Is Born*. Garden City, NY: Doubleday, 1978.

Jeffers, Susan. *All the Pretty Horses*. New York: Macmillan, 1974.

Jensen, Patricia. *The Mess*. Chicago: Children's Press, 1990.

Jeram, Judson. *I Never Saw . . .* New York: Whitman, 1974.

Jewell, Nancy. *ABC Cat*. New York: Harper, 1983.

Johnson, Crockett. *A Picture for Harold's Room*. New York: Harper & Row, 1968.

——. *Harold at the North Pole*. New York: Harper & Row, 1958.

Johnson, Lee & Sue Kaiser Johnson. *If I Ran The Family*. Minneapolis, MN: Free Spirit, 1992.

Johnson, Odette & Bruce Johnson. *Rainbows Under the Sea*. Oxford Press, 1993.

Johnston, Tony. *Three Little Bikers*. New York: Knopf, 1994.

——. *The Quilt Story*. New York: Putnam's Sons, 1985.

——. *Yonder*. New York: Puffin, 1988.

——. *Five Little Foxes and the Snow*. New York: Putnam, 1977.

Jonas, Ann. *Where Can It Be?* New York: Greenwillow, 1986.

——. *When You Were a Baby*. New York: Penguin/Puffin, 1986.

Joosse, Barbara. *Mama, Do You Love Me?* New York: Scholastic, 1991.

Jorgensen, Gail. *Crocodile Beat*. New York: Bradbury, 1989.

Joslin, Sesyle. *What Do You Do, Dear?* New York: Young Scott, 1961.

——. *What Do You Say, Dear?* Reading, MA: Addison-Wesley, 1958.

Joyce, William. *George Shrinks*. New York: Harper & Row, 1987.

Koontz, Robin Michal

I See Something You Don't See

Illustrated by the author
Cobblehill/Dutton, 1992. ISBN: 0-525-65077-6

Annotation

Two children are spending a summer day with their grandmother. During their stay, they play a guessing game trying to out-riddle one another. Each riddle begins the same way, "Riddle-me, riddle-me-ree, I see something you don't see." Then clues are given. The object being described is hidden in the picture on the right-hand page. An answer key is provided in the back of the book.

Innovation

Suggest that children create their own rhyme to go with the opening chant. Each riddle could include at least two descriptors. They could also hide their object in a picture they draw. You might want to use some of the suggestions listed on pages 12 and 13 and the frame shown here.

> *Riddle-me*
> *Riddle-me-ree*
> *I see something*
>   *you don't see.*
> *It's something _____.*
> *It's something _____.*

Cross-Curricular Activities

The Arts: Suggest that children sing the first part of the riddle, stopping to let each child show a page with the original part of the riddle. You might want to write out the music the children create so that it is large enough for all to see. On the other hand, you might want to simply strum the guitar or some other instrument as the students "sing" the first part of the riddle.

Reading: Reread the book asking students to identify rhyming words on each page. Then have them identify rhyming words in their own riddles.

Science: If students are learning about certain animals or foods, you might have them create a riddle page with an accompanying picture for a creature they select. This could serve as an excellent culminating activity for a given unit.

Social Studies: Ask children to tell about what they like to do when they go to their grandparents' house or what they like to play with brothers, sisters, or friends. What makes the games fun? Do the games ever cause arguments? If so, how do they resolve any disagreements?

Kroll, Virginia

New Friends, True Friends, Stuck-Like-Glue Friends

Illustrated by Rose Rosely
William B. Eerdman's, 1994. ISBN: 0-8028-5085-5

Annotation

Friends do many things together as this book well illustrates. They lounge by pools, share hugs, go to meetings, and take walks while eating ice cream. These are a few of the several activities mentioned in this book.

Innovation

Ask children what they like to do with their friends. Then suggest that they create their own "best friends" book. Like Kroll's book, their books could focus on doing things. You might want to provide students with the frame shown below to get them started. Also see suggestions listed on pages 12 and 13.

Things Friends Do

Cross-Curricular Activities

Language Arts: Have students identify the rhyming words used in the book. Once identified, divide the class into groups. Give each group one set of rhyming words. Have each group see how many additional words they can create to rhyme with each set of rhyming words. Have each group share their lists.

Social Studies: Have students talk about what they consider to be qualities of friends. What kinds of things do they do with their friends? What do they try to do to make friends?

Kuskin, Karla

City Noise

Illustrated by Renee Flower
HarperCollins, 1994. ISBN: 0-06-021076-1

Annotation

A child living in the inner city discovers an old tin can. Pretending that it is a conch shell, he puts it next to his ear. Several sounds of a busy city such as honking, laughing and machines, are revealed to him.

Innovation

Ask students to think of the sounds they hear when they are in different places. Schedule a field trip. On the field trip ask children to use their hands cupped over their ears to detect the sounds they hear. Once back in the room, suggest that they create their own "noises book." Like Kuskin's book, each page could be devoted to a different noise. Also see pages 12 and 13 for additional innovation suggestions.

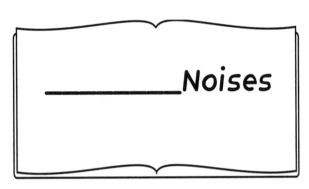

Cross-Curricular Activities

The Arts: Write each action word on a card and place each in a "mystery bag." Have a student take one card out of the bag and pantomime the word.

Language Arts: This book is filled with verbs. You might want to call students' attention to all of the action words by listing them and asking how all of the words are alike. Write the words *Action Words* in the center of the board or chart paper. Ask students to think of other actions they see people do in the city. Write their responses around the center.

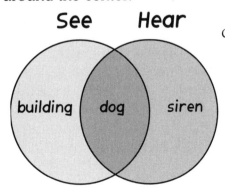

Science: For a likenesses/differences activity, have children fill out a Venn diagram similar to the one shown here. Write *See* above the circle to the left and *Hear* above the circle to the right. Then have children name an object for a given place such as the city. If they can "see" it, have them write it on the *See* side. If they can "hear" it, have them write it on the *Hear* side. If they can both see and hear it, have them write it in the center where the circles overlap.

Additional *K*'s

Kafka, Sherry. *I Need A Friend*. New York: Putnam's Sons, 1971.

Kahn, Joan. *You Can't Catch Me*. New York: Harper & Row, 1976.

Kalan, Robert. *Jump, Frog, Jump!* New York: Scholastic, 1981.

——. *Rain*. New York: Scholastic, 1978.

Keats, Ezra Jack. *Over in the Meadow*. New York: Scholastic, 1971.

Keller, Holly. *Will It Rain?* New York: Greenwillow, 1984.

——. *Too Big*. New York: Greenwillow, 1983.

Kellog, Steven. *Can I Keep Him?* New York: Dial, 1971.

Kent, Jack. *Silly Goose*. Englewood Cliffs, NJ: Prentice-Hall, 1983.

——. *The Fat Cat*. New York: Scholastic, 1971.

Kesselman, Wendy. *There's a Train Going by My Window*. Garden City, NY: Doubleday, 1982.

Kessler, Ethel & Leonard Kessler. *What's Inside the Box?* New York: Scholastic, 1976.

——. *Do Baby Bears Sit in Chairs?* Garden City, NY: Doubleday, 1961.

Kessler, Leonard. *Hey Diddle Diddle*. New York: Garrard, 1980.

——. *Do You Have Any Carrots?* Champaign, IL: Garrard, 1979.

Kherdian, David. *Right Now*. New York: Knopf, 1983.

Killion, Bette. *The Same Wind*. New York: HarperCollins, 1992.

King, Christopher. *The Vegetables Go to Bed*. New York: Crown, 1994.

Kingman, Lee. *Catch the Baby*. New York: Puffin, 1990.

Kirk, David. *Miss Spider's Tea Party*. New York: Scholastic, 1994.

Kitchen, Bert. *When Hunger Calls*. Candlewick, 1994.

Klein, Leonore. *Only One Ant*. New York: Hastings House, 1971.

——. *Silly Sam*. New York: Scholastic, 1969.

——. *Brave Daniel*. New York: Scholastic, 1958.

Kline, Suzy. *Don't Touch!* Niles, IL: Whiman, 1985.

Knowles, Sheena. *Edward the Emu*. New York: HarperCollins, 1990.

Komaiko, Leah. *Where Can It Be?* New York: Orchard, 1994.

——. *Great Aunt Ida and Her Great Dane, Doc*. New York: Doubleday, 1994.

——. *Earl's Too Cool for Me*. New York: HarperCollins, 1988.

Kowalezyk, Carolyn. *Purple Is Part of a Rainbow*. Chicago: Children's Press, 1985.

Krasilovsky, Phyllis. *The Man Who Didn't Wash His Dishes*. New York: Scholastic, 1982.

——. *Milton the Early Riser*. Harmondsworth, UK: Puffin, 1976.

——. *Leo the Late Bloomer*. New York: HarperCollins, 1971.

——. *Whose Mouse Are You?* New York: Scholastic, 1970.

Kraus, Ruth. *I Can Fly*. New York: Golden Press, 1985.

——. *The Happy Egg*. New York: Scholastic, 1983.

——. *Is This You?* New York: Scholastic, 1955.

——. *Bears*. New York: Scholastic, 1948.

——. *The Carrot Seed*. New York: Scholastic, 1945.

Kudrna, C. Imbior. *To Battle a Boa*. Minneapolis, MN: Carolrhoda, 1986.

Kuskin, Karla. *Patchwork Island*. New York: HarperCollins, 1994.

——. *Just Like Everyone Else*. New York: Harper & Row, 1982.

Kwitz, Mary DeBall. *Little Chick's Story*. New York: Harper & Row, 1978.

Lankford, Mary

Is It Dark? Is It Light?

Illustrated by Stacey Schuett
Knopf, 1991. ISBN: 0-679-81579-1

Annotation

Two children ask questions about the "it" and provide the reader with a lesson in opposites, too. At the end of the book, we see that the "it" is really the moon, answering the final question, "What is it?" The author also conveys the wonderment of the moon felt by children all over the world by showing children of many cultures and the word they use for *moon* on the last two pages. The book closes with a listing of the different languages that are shown and the translation for *moon* in each language.

Innovation

Suggest that children create their own "What is it?" books by thinking of an object they would like to describe. Using the frame shown here might be of help as might the suggestions listed on pages 12 and 13.

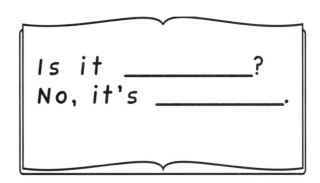

Cross-Curricular Activities

Language Arts: Reread the book with the students, asking them to identify the objects in the pictures that represent the opposites. You might then want to write each pair of opposites on a piece of paper and have students identify a magazine picture that represents the pair. Each picture could be affixed to the paper. Students could also create their own book of opposites by thinking of additional words that are opposites, writing each on facing pages, and illustrating or finding pictures for each pair.

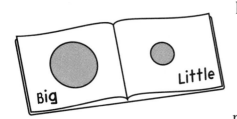

Science: If students are learning about a subject such as the solar system, animals, or plants, you might want to have them choose a given example from the category and create a "What is it?" book. The frame shown above (see Innovation) could be used, and students could reveal the answer on the last page. This would be a way to review or could be used as a "mini" report in which students would have to discover more about their particular word. Their opposite clues would provide evidence of their new-found knowledge.

Note: You might also want to use this book to emphasize different languages.

Lindbergh, Reeve
What Is the Sun?

Illustrated by Stephen Lambert
Candlewick, 1994. ISBN: 1-56402-146-7

Annotation

A grandson has several questions about the sun, moon, tide, wind, and rain and his grandmother tries to answer them as she tucks him into bed. She provides facts about each, and these are written in poetic fashion. The pictures show the boy and his dog exploring the world as each question is asked and answered.

Innovation

Allow students to talk and ask questions about other things in nature. Write each question as they ask it. Then suggest that they find answers to each question and create their own "What" books using the questions and answers. The frame below might be of help as might the suggestions on pages 12 and 13.

What is the ____?
The ____ is ____.

Cross-Curricular Activities

Language Arts: This book lends itself to partner-reading. Divide children into pairs. Have one child read the question, the other read the answer. You might also want to do this as a whole class activity, dividing the class into two parts. One part reads the questions; the other reads the statements. You could also use this book to teach students about the differences between questions and statements. Point out the different punctuation marks and the way the voice is used with each.

Science: Divide students into pairs. Have each pair choose one animal or another nature-related object that you are studying. Ask them to write a question and statement about their selected object.

Loban, Anita

Away from Home

Illustrated by the author
Greenwillow, 1994. ISBN: 0-688-10354-5

Annotation

Alliteration is used to help readers learn about different places around the world and about the alphabet. A city in an exotic place is named for each letter of the alphabet as is a character and his/her action. For example, the book begins, "Adam arrived in Amsterdam." The book ends with a list of all the cities mentioned, where they are located, and one interesting fact about each city.

Innovation

Talk with children about places to which they have traveled. Then suggest that they create one page for a class travel book using their names. The frame shown at the right might be of help as might the suggestions on pages 12 and 13.

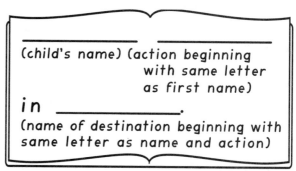

(child's name) (action beginning with same letter as first name)

in _____.
(name of destination beginning with same letter as name and action)

Cross-Curricular Activities

Language Arts: Use this book to teach alphabetical order. On cards write the names of characters, places each traveled, and/or the actions they used to get to the city and have students alphabetize the cards according to the first letter. You could also point out that names of people and cities begin with capital letters by having children use the cards to reconstruct the sentences in the pocket holder and calling their attention to the way the words begin.

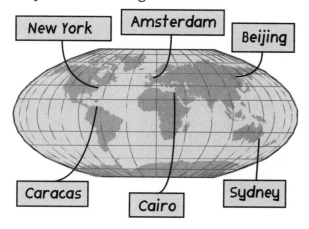

New York   Amsterdam   Beijing
Caracas   Cairo   Sydney

Social Studies: Place a map showing the various cities on a bulletin board. Write the name of each city on a card and place the cards around the map, attaching a piece of string or yarn to each. Show children where each city is located by using a pin to connect the piece of string or yarn to the correct place on the map.

Another social studies-related activity involves teaching the students about the term *cities*. Just what is a city? After listing specific attributes, perhaps students could be expected to find out one interesting detail about their city. These could be compiled into a class book; the title should include a descriptive word that begins with the same letter as the name of the city.

Additional *L*'s

Lacome, Julie. *I'm a Jolly Farmer*. Cambridge: Candlewick, 1994.

—. *Walking Through the Jungle*. Cambridge: Candlewick, 1993.

Langstaff, John. *Oh, A-Hunting We Will Go*. New York: Atheneum, 1974.

—. *The Golden Vanity*. New York: Harcourt Brace, 1972.

—. *Soldier, Soldier, Won't You Marry Me?* New York: Doubleday, 1972.

Laurence, Ester. *We're Off to Catch a Dragon*. Nashville, TN: Abington, 1969.

Lear, Edward. *Whizz!* New York: Macmillan, 1973.

Leemis, Ralph. *Mister Momboo's Hat*. New York: Dutton, 1991.

Lenski, Lois. *Susie Mariar*. Walck, 1967.

LeSeig, Theo. *In a People House*. New York: Random House, 1972.

Lester, Alison. *Clive Eats Alligators*. New York: Scholastic, 1985.

Lester, Helen. *It Wasn't My Fault*. Boston: Houghton Mifflin, 1985.

Leuck, Laura. *Sun Is Falling, Night Is Calling*. New York: Simon & Schuster, 1994.

Levinson, Riki. *I Go with My Family to Grandma's*. New York: Dutton, 1986.

Lewis, Bobby. *Home Before Midnight*. New York: Lothrop, 1984.

Lewison, Wendy. *Buzz Said the Bee*. New York: Scholastic, 1992.

—. *Going to Sleep on the Farm*. New York: Dial, 1992.

—. *Mud*. New York: Random House, 1990.

Lexau, Joan. *Crocodile and Hen*. New York: Harper & Row, 1969.

Leydenfirst, Robert. *Ten Little Elephants*. Garden City, NY: Doubleday, 1975.

—. *The Snake That Sneezed!* New York: Putnam's Sons, 1970.

Lillegard, Dee. *Sitting in My Box*. New York: Puffin Unicorn, 1989.

Lillie, Patricia. *When the Rooster Crowed*. New York: Greenwillow, 1991.

Lindbergh, Anne. *Tidy Lady*. New York: Harcourt Brace, 1989.

Lindbergh, Reeve. *Grandfather's Lovesong*. New York: Viking, 1993.

—. *There's a Cow in the Road*. New York: Dial, 1993.

—. *Benjamin's Barn*. New York: Puffin-Pied Piper, 1990.

Lionni, Leo. *Inch by Inch*. New York: Scholastic, 1994.

—. *Little Blue and Little Yellow*. New York: Scholastic, 1993.

Lipson, Michael. *How the Wind Plays*. New York: Hyperion, 1994.

Littledale, Freya. *The Magic Fish*. New York: Scholastic, 1967.

Livermore, Elaine. *Three Little Kittens Lost Their Mittens*. Boston: Houghton Mifflin, 1979.

—. *One to Ten, Count Again*. Boston: Houghton Mifflin, 1973.

Lobel, Anita. *The Pancake*. New York: Greenwillow, 1978.

Lobel, Arnold. *The Rose in My Garden*. New York: Scholastic, 1984.

—. *On Market Street*. New York: Greenwillow, 1981.

Long, Earlene. *Gone Fishing*. Boston: Houghton Mifflin, 1987.

Lorenz, Lee. *Big Gus and Little Gus*. New York: Prentice-Hall, 1982.

Low, Joseph. *My Dog, Your Dog*. New York: Macmillan, 1978.

Lubin, Leonard B. *This Little Pig*. New York: Lothrop, Lee & Shepard, 1985.

Lyon, George Ella. *The Outside Inn*. New York: Orchard, 1991.

—. *Together*. New York: Macmillan/McGraw-Hill, 1989.

Martin, Bill

Polar Bear, Polar Bear What Do You Hear?

Illustrated by Eric Carle
Henry Holt, 1991. ISBN: 0-8050-1759-3

Annotation

Various zoo animals make their sounds for one another throughout this book. A review of all the animals and their sounds appears at the end when the zookeeper states that he hears children making the sounds associated with each animal. This book is written with the same pattern as Martin's *Brown Bear, Brown Bear, What Do You See?*

Innovation

Have children provide names of other animals and the sounds each makes. Suggest that they make their own books about these animals and sounds using the same pattern as Martin. The frame shown here might be of help as might the suggestions listed on pages 12 and 13.

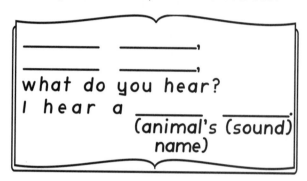

Cross-Curricular Activities

The Arts: Have children use a large paper bag and other art supplies to create a mask that represents one of the animals in the story. Once constructed, have children retell the story with children wearing masks for the given animals; they stand when their animal is mentioned.

Science: Have children learn about a given category of animals. For example, you might have them learn about animals of the rain forest. Then have them create their book to represent these animals and their sounds. You might want to have different groups of children working with different groups of animals. Their books could be placed in the "reference" section of your classroom library.

McDonnell, Flora

I Love Animals

Illustrated by the author
Candlewick, 1994. ISBN: 1-56402-387-7

Annotation

A little girl names all of the farm animals she likes. As she does this, she tells one thing in particular that she loves about each animal. The book ends with her statement that she loves all the animals and, of course, that they love her, too!

Innovation

Ask children to name animals that they love and one particular action that they most love about the animal. Suggest that they create their own books using the frame below. Additional suggestions for publishing innovations are shown on pages 12 and 13.

I love _____.
(state why – one particular thing or action)

Cross-Curricular Activities

The Arts: This book lends itself to learning about action words. You might want to have students pantomime each action mentioned in the story. They could do this as a whole class, or you could have given students represent the different animals and act out their part when mentioned in the rereading of the story.

Language Arts: Reread the book, stopping after each page to ask children what the animal did— the action or movement. Then, ask the children to tell other actions the given animals often do.

Miranda, Anne

Does a Mouse Have a House?

Illustrated by the author
Bradbury, 1994. ISBN: 0-02-76251-4

Annotation

This book is about 17 animals and their natural habitats. Told in rhyme, each page names one animal and its home. The book ends with an answer to the question posed by the title, showing a mouse making a nest in the grass.

Innovation

After talking about the animals mentioned in the book, suggest that students create their own two-sentence rhymes about an animal of their choice. Suggestions for ways to publish their innovations are listed on pages 12 and 13. The basic frame shown below could be used.

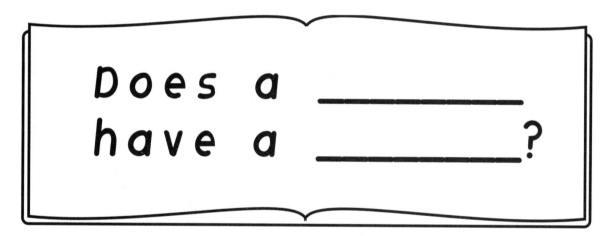

Cross-Curricular Activities

The Arts/Science: Have students choose an animal from the story. Then give each child a shoebox and other art supplies and have children create the habitat for their animal. Finally, have them use clay to model their animal and place it in the diorama.

Language Arts: This book lends itself to meaningful association with rhyming words. Copy each set of phrases onto sentence strips, leaving a blank for the word that rhymes with the one in the first part of the sentence. Line this up so that the blank is under the word to be rhymed. Begin reading the phrase, asking children to read with you. Ask them to help you fill in the missing word and to watch as you write it. Ask them what they notice about the words that rhyme. Are they spelled similarly? What makes them rhyme?

Additional *M's*

Mack, Stan. *10 Bears in My Bed*. New York: Patheon, 1974.

Maestro, Betsy & Giulio Maestro. *Traffic, A Book of Opposites*. New York: Crown, 1981.

Mandel, Peter. *Red Cat, White Cat*. New York: Henry Holt, 1994.

Mansell, Dom. *My Old Teddy*. Cambridge, MA: Candlewick, 1992.

Maris, Ron. *Is Anyone Home?* New York: Greenwillow, 1985.

——. *Are You There, Bear?* New York: Greenwillow, 1984.

——. *My Book*. New York: Puffin, 1983.

Marshall, Janet Perry. *Oh My Gosh My Pocket*. Honesdale, PA: Bell, 1992.

Martin, Bill. *The Wizard*. New York: Harcourt Brace, 1994.

——. *Brown Bear, Brown Bear*. New York: Holt, 1970.

Martin, Bill & John Archambault. *Listen to the Rain*. New York: Holt: 1988.

Martin, Linda. *When Dinosaurs Go Visiting*. San Fransico: Chronicle, 1993.

Masurel, Claire & Marie Henry. *Good Night*. San Francisco: Chronicle, 1993.

Matthias, Catherine. *Over-Under*. Chicago: Children's Press, 1984.

Mayer, Mercer. *I Was So Mad*. New York: Golden Press, 1983.

——. *What Do You Do with a Kangaroo?* New York: Scholastic, 1973.

McAllister, Angela. *Sleepy Ella*. New York: Doubleday, 1994.

McClintok, Mike. *A Fly Went By*. New York: Random House, 1958.

McDaniel, Becky B. *Katie Did It*. Chicago: Chidren's Press, 1983.

McGovern, Ann. *Too Much Noise*. New York: Scholastic, 1967.

McKee, David. *I Hate My Teddy Bear*. New York: Clarion, 1982.

McKissack, Patricia C. *Who Is Who?* Chicago: Children's Press, 1983.

McLeish, Kenneth. *Chiken Licken*. Scarsdale, NY: Bradbury, 1973.

McMillan, Bruce. *Play Day: A Book of Terse Verse*. New York: Holiday, 1991.

McPhail, David. *Pigs Aplenty, Pigs Galore!* New York: Scholastic, 1993.

Melmed, Laura Krauss. *I Love You As Much...* New York: Lothrop, Lee & Shepard, 1993.

Memling, Carl. *Ten Little Animals*. New York: Golden Press, 1961.

Merriam, Eve. *Do You Want to See Something?* New York: Scholastic, 1965.

Micklethwait, Lucy. *I Spy a Lion: Animals in Art*. New York: Greenwillow, 1994.

Miller, Jane. *Farm Noises*. New York: Simon & Schuster, 1989.

Miller, Margaret. *Guess Who?* New York: Greenwillow, 1994.

——. *My Five Senses*. New York: Simon & Schuster, 1994.

——. *Can You Guess?* New York: Greenwillow, 1993.

——. *Who Uses This?* New York: Greenwillow, 1990.

Moffett, Martha. *A Flower Pot Is Not a Hat*. New York: Dutton, 1972.

Moncure, Jane B. *Animal, Animal, Where Do You Live?* Chicago: Children's Press, 1975.

Moore, Lilian. *I'll Meet You at The Cucumbers*. New York: Atheneum, 1988.

Morgenstern, Constance. *Good Night, Feet*. New York: Holt, 1991.

Morozumi, Aksuko. *One Gorilla*. New York: Farrar, Straus, & Giroux, 1990.

Morris, Ann. *Bread Bread Bread*. New York: Lothrop, 1989.

——. *Hats Hats Hats*. New York: Lothrop, Lee & Shepard, 1989.

Most, Bernard. *If the Dinosaurs Came Back*. New York: Harcourt Brace, 1978.

Munsch, Robert. *Love You Forever*. Willowdale, Ontario: Firefly, 1986.

Neitzel, Shirley
The Jacket I Wear in the Snow

Illustrated by Nancy Winslow Parker
Mulberry, 1989. ISBN: 0-688-08028-6

Annotation

This is a cumulative tale about a girl who tells about a jacket she wears when she plays in the snow. She begins by showing and telling about the whole coat. On succeeding pages she tells about the many parts of her coat, mentioning one new part on every page and repeating the parts previously mentioned. Pictures are used for some of the words – rebus style.

Innovation

Ask children to think of another piece of clothing they wear that has several parts. Suggest that they create their own books using a pattern similar to Neitzel's.

> This is the
> _____ I wear
> in the _____.

Cross-Curricular Activities

Health: Brainstorm with students the type of clothing that is needed for given weather conditions. You might want to create a large semantic map to go with your discussion. Write *Weather Conditions* in the center. Have children first think of and state the conditions, then the types of clothes needed for each condition. Write their suggestions to create the semantic web.

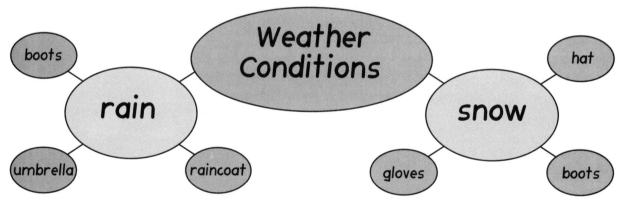

Language Arts: This book lends itself well to choral reading where each child has an opportunity to participate. After copying the various lines onto sentence strips, give each child a strip. Have them sit in a circle in order, so that once the reading begins you'll be able to keep the flow. When a new line is read, a child reads solo. However, the whole class is expected to read the repeated lines. As the story progresses, then, the whole class will end up reading the story!

Nerlove, Miriam
If All the World Were Paper

Illustrated by the author
Whitman, 1991. ISBN: 0-8075-3535-4

Annotation

If you could use your imagination, some paper, a paintbrush, and some paints, what would you put in your world? The boy in this book will give you some ideas as he uses all of these to create his colorful world. Giving himself wings to fly with the clouds is one example of many provided in the book.

Innovation

Ask children what they would do if given the same materials as the boy in the story. Suggest that they write their own "If" books using the frame shown below. Each child could create one page for a class book that could begin and end with the first four lines of Nerlove's book. The suggestions on pages 12 and 13 offer additional ways to publish children's innovations.

Cross-Curricular Activities

The Arts: Provide children with watercolors and have them paint pictures of their imaginary worlds. The illustrations of this book show how colors are formed by adding additional colors. Knowing this, you might want to do a lesson on primary and secondary colors. Provide students with directions so that they can create the various colors. Have students use food coloring, eyedroppers, and water. Have them place a few drops of food coloring into the water and note what happens.

Language Arts: Have children identify the many words that rhyme. Write each on a card as they identify it. On a third card, write the word part that is the same for a given pair of words. Pass out the word cards to the students. Place one of the word family cards in the pocket holder. The students holding word cards containing the same word family place their cards in the pocket holder right under the word family card. Point out likenesses and differences.

Nodset, Joan

Who Took the Farmer's Hat?

Illustrated by Fritz Siebel
Scholastic, 1963. ISBN:0-590-02950-9

Annotation

A farmer loses his favorite hat while he is working on the farm. The wind blows it around and by several animals. As the farmer searches for his hat, he asks each animal the same question, "Have you seen my hat?" Although the animals have seen it, they don't realize it. They think it's something else which is what they tell the farmer. At long last he climbs the tree to take a look at a bird's nest and discovers his hat.

Innovation

Ask students to name another object the farmer might lose. They might also like to think of another person who could lose something. Suggest that they write about their ideas using a similar pattern. They might want to have the farmer ask different animals in their books. The frame shown here could be used, as could some of the suggestions on pages 12 and 13.

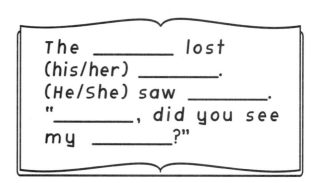

The _____ lost
(his/her) _____.
(He/She) saw _____.
"_____, did you see
my _____?"

Cross-Curricular Activities

The Arts: This book helps the reader to see that given a little imagination, an object can be used for more than one thing. Provide each student with an object, such as a small empty box, and other art supplies. Ask them to create something with their box. You could also ask them to identify an object at home or in the classroom that could be used for more than its one intended purpose. For example, a milk carton could be used for holding paintbrushes.

Language Arts: Write the name of each animal on a paper plate. Attach a piece of string or yarn long enough so that the plate can be slipped over a student's head. Assign selected students the characters. One child is also the farmer. Begin telling the story, having characters read their lines when it's their turn.

Science: Have children discuss why the wind was able to carry the hat away. Are there other objects that the wind could/couldn't carry away? Perhaps you could make a list of "coulds" and "couldn'ts."

Additional *N*'s

Namm, Diane. *Little Bear*. Chicago: Children's Press, 1990.

Narahashi, Keiko. *Is That Josie?* New York: Macmillan, 1994.

Nash, Ogden. *The Adventures of Isabel*. Boston: Little Brown, 1991.

——. *The Animal Garden*. New York: Lippincott, 1963.

Nave, Yolanda. *Goosebumps and Butterflies*. New York: Watts, 1990.

Neitzel, Shirley. *The Dress I'll Wear to the Party*. New York: Greenwillow, 1992.

Neasi, Barbara J. *Just Like Me*. Chicago: Children's Press, 1984.

Nerlove, Miriam. *Just One Tooth*. New York: Macmillan, 1989.

——. *I Meant to Clean My Room Today*. New York: Macmillan, 1988.

——. *I Made a Mistake*. New York: Atheneum, 1985.

Newsome, Carol. *An Edward Lear Alphabet*. New York: Lothrop, Lee, & Shepard, 1983.

Nic Leodhas, Sorche. *All in The Morning Early*. New York: Holt, 1963.

Nightingale, Sandy. *A Giraffe on the Moon*. New York: Harcourt Brace, 1991.

Nims, Bonnie. *Where Is the Bear at School?* New York: Whitman, 1989.

——. *Where Is the Bear?* New York: Whitman, 1988.

Nixon, Joan L. *If You Say So, Claude*. New York: Warne, 1980.

Noble, Trinka Hakes. *The Day Jimmy's Boa Ate the Wash*. New York: Scholastic, 1980.

——. *The King's Tea*. New York: Dial, 1979.

Nolan, Dennis. *Wizard McBean and His Flying Machine*. Englewood Cliffs, NJ: Prentice-Hall, 1977.

——. *Big Pig*. Englewood Cliffs, NJ: Prentice-Hall, 1977.

Noll, Sally. *Lucky Morning*. New York: Greenwillow, 1994.

——. *Off and Counting*. New York: Greenwillow, 1984.

Novak, Matt. *Mouse TV*. New York: Orchard, 1994.

Noyes, Alfred. *The Highwayman*. New York: Harcourt Brace, 1990.

Numeroff, Laura Joffe. *Dogs Don't Wear Sneakers*. New York: Simon & Schuster, 1993.

——. *If You Give a Moose a Muffin*. New York: HarperCollins, 1991.

——. *If You Give a Mouse a Cookie*. New York: Harper & Row, 1985.

O'Keefe, Susan Heyboer

One Hungry Monster

Illustrated by Lynn Munsinger
Little, Brown, 1989. ISBN: 0-316-63388-7

Annotation

A young boy can't sleep because monsters keep multiplying and begging to be fed. Finally, after ten monsters the boy has had enough and prepares a dinner for them. However, instead of eating the food the boy brings to them, they play with it, making a real mess. Totally fed up, the boy hollers at them and demands that they leave the house. Once rid of them, he eats an apple muffin, one item the monsters didn't find!

Innovation

After having students recall the monsters and the food the boy tried to fix for them, suggest that they create their own "hungry monster" books. They could make it a number book similar to O'Keefe's. Instead of having each child create a book, you could use the suggestions listed on pages 12 and 13 and have them create a class or group book.

Cross-Curricular Activities

The Arts: Provide children with construction paper scraps and invite them to create their own monsters.

Mathematics: Both number words and numerals are used in this book. Have each student make a set of cards to be used with this book. On one side of the card, have them write a number word. On the reverse side, have them write the corresponding numeral. Ask students to spread their cards out in front of them. Reread the book. When you come to a number word, have them hold up the matching numeral card. When you come to a numeral, have them hold up the matching word.

Ormerod, Jan

101 Things to Do With a Baby

Illustrated by the author
Mulberry, 1984. ISBN: 0-688-127703

Annotation

A young girl tells what she can do with her baby brother. In fact, she comes up with about 101 different things. Each page is filled with pictures that are numbered and labeled, showing each idea for using a baby brother.

Innovation

Review the many things that the girl did with her baby brother and ask students if they have any additional ideas. Then suggest that they think of an object and of the many things that could be done with their chosen object. You might want to provide them with this basic frame for their titles.

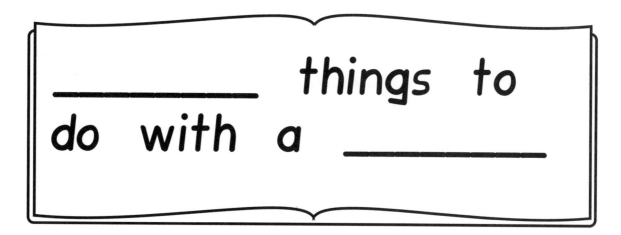

Cross-Curricular Activities

Mathematics: Use this book to help children see the repetitive nature of our number system. After counting to 101, ask them what they think will come next. Why do they think so? How would the number be written?

Social Studies: Have children talk about families. What makes a family? How many family members do they have? What kinds of things do they do with their family members?

Oxenbury, Helen
It's My Birthday

Illustrated by the author
Candlewick, 1993. ISBN: 1-56402-412-1

Annotation

A child is having a birthday, and the animal friends want to help make a birthday cake. Each animal friend brings a different ingredient for the cake. Through repetition, the reader learns about the necessary ingredients for making a cake.

Innovation

Ask children to think of another special occasion and what they might like to make if they could. Suggest that they create a book to tell about their day and what they will prepare for it. How many people will help? You might want to have them use the frame shown at right.

It's my _____
and I'm going to _____.
I need _____.
"I'll get you some _____,"
said the _____.

Cross-Curricular Activities

Social Studies: Ask children what they do on their birthdays. Any special activities? Do they have a cake? If so, what kind? Do they receive cards? Suggest that they make a birthday card that can be given to a class member.

Mathematics: Bring in all necessary utensils, ingredients, and a recipe for making a cake. Print the recipe on chart paper large enough for all to see. Have students create the cake following the recipe. Point out measurements and the necessity of following the directions in the order stated.

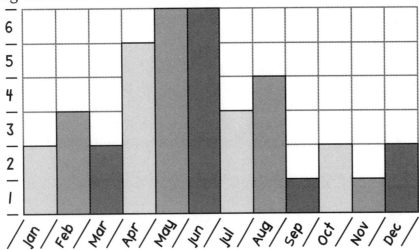

Another math activity involves graphing. Create a bar graph that has a column for each month. Ask children to tell when their birthday is by coloring in a square in the correct column.

Additional *O*'s

O'Conner, Jane. *The Teeny Tiny Woman*. New York: Random House, 1986.

Ochs, Carol. *Moose on the Loose*. Minneapolis: Carolrhoda Books, 1991.

O'Donnell, Elizabeth. *The Twelve Days of Summer*. New York: Morrow, 1991.

O'Huigin, Sean. *King of the Birds*. Firefly, 1991.

Olsen, Ib. *The Grown-up Trap*. Thomasson-Grant, 1992.

O'Neill, Mary. *Big Red Hen*. Garden City, NY: Doubleday, 1971.

Oppenheim, Joanne. *Donkey's Tale*. New York: Bantam, 1991.

——. *Left and Right*. New York: Harcourt Brace, 1989.

——. *"Not Now!" Said the Cow*. New York: Bantam, 1989.

——. *The Storybook Prince*. New York: Harcourt Brace, 1987.

——. *Have You Seen Birds?* New York: Scholastic, 1986.

——. *You Can't Catch Me*. Boston: Houghton Mifflin, 1986.

——. *Have You Seen Roads?* New York: Addison-Wesley, 1969.

——. *Have You Seen Trees?* New York: Young Scott, 1967.

Orbach, Ruth. *Apple Pigs*. New York: Philomel, 1981.

Orgel, Doris. *Merry Merry February*. Parents Magazine Press, 1978.

Ormerod, Jan. *Come Back, Kittens*. New York: Lothrop, Lee & Shepard, 1992.

——. *When We Went to the Zoo*. New York: Lothrop, Lee & Shepard, 1990.

Otto, Carolyn. *Dinosaur Chase*. New York: HarperCollins, 1991.

——. *Ducks, Ducks, Ducks*. New York: HarperCollins, 1991.

Owen, Roy. *My Night Forest*. New York: Four Winds Press, 1994.

Owens, Mary Beth. *A Caribou Alphabet*. New York: Farrar, Strauss & Giroux, 1990.

Oxenbury, Helen. *Pig Tale*. New York: Morrow, 1974.

Paschkis, Julie

So Sleepy, Wide Awake

Illustrated by the author
Henry Holt, 1994. ISBN: 0-8050-3174-X

Annotation

This book really tells two stories, each printed in the opposite direction. The first story is all about sleeping animals, with the pictures showing just how they sleep. A flip of the book reveals the second story which is about awakened animals. Descriptive verbs such as *slithers*, *flutters*, and *slumbers* are used.

Innovation

Children might like to tell how other animals sleep and the actions they perform when awake. Suggest that they use these to create yet another book about animals. You could also suggest that they create an "asleep/awake" book about the city or farm. See pages 12 and 13 for publishing innovations.

> All of the _____ are so sleepy. (Change to awake halfway through.)
> The _____ _____.

Cross-Curricular Activities

The Arts: Have children create their own block prints. Have them cut a shape into a sponge, dip the sponge into paint, and make prints!

Language Arts: Ask children to name the actions of the animals. Why do they suppose the author used these words? Were they more interested in the story because the author used these words? Could they better picture what the animal was doing?

Phillips, Louis

The Upside Down Riddle Book

Illustrated by Beau Gardner
Lothrop, Lee & Shepard, 1982. ISBN: 0-688-00931-X

Annotation

This is a book of riddles in which the riddle is provided on the left-hand side, the answer on the facing page. The riddle is in words. However, the answer is in picture form – upside down, no less!

Innovation

Invite children to create their own riddle books, using rhyme and pictures as did Phillips. This could be an individual or class project. See pages 12 and 13 for additional suggestions.

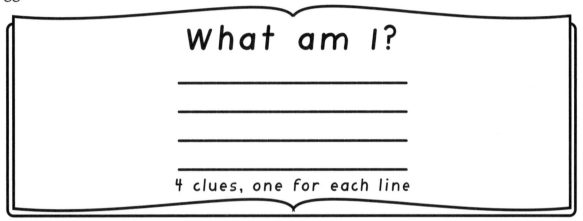

What am I?

_____
_____
_____

_____

4 clues, one for each line

Cross-Curricular Activities

The Arts: Have students learn more about figure/ground by having them create pictures using a technique similar to the one used in the book. Provide each of them with two different sheets of construction paper. Instruct them to create a picture on one of the pieces of paper, cut it out, and affix it to the other whole sheet of paper.

Science: Ask students to create accordion riddles for a given subject. They need three clues, one of which is written on each fold. The answer is on the back of the last fold.

Protopopescu, Orel

The Perilous Pit

Illustrated by Jaqueline Chwast
Simon & Schuster, 1993. ISBN: 0-671-76910-3

Annotation

A girl sits under a peach tree reading a book and eating a peach. When finished with the peach, she throws the pit over her shoulder without looking up from her book. The pit causes a series of events, only to cycle back to the girl picking up another peach, eating it, and tossing the pit.

Innovation

Suggest that students create their own "circular" tale beginning with the frame shown below.

```
One _____ day
_____ sat under a _____ tree
reading a book and eating a _____.
And when _____ got down
to the last bite,
_____ threw away the _____.
```

Cross-Curricular Activities

Language Arts: Help students to see the structure that was used to write this story by writing each event on a sentence strip. Then create a circle on the floor using a rope. Place the events around the circle as the story is retold.

Science: Bring in a tree branch and stand it upright in a bucket of sand or rocks. Ask students to name other trees that bear fruit. Write each name on a shape resembling the fruit and hang each on the tree.

Additional *P*'s

Pack, Robert. *Then What Did You Do?* New York: Macmillan, 1961.

Packard, Mary. *The Kite.* Chicago: Children's Press, 1990.

Pare, Roger. *Animal Capers.* Firefly, 1992.

Parr, Letitia. *A Man and His Hat.* New York: Putnam, 1991.

Palmer, Helen. *Why I Built the Boogle House.* New York: Random House, 1964.

Parker, John. *I Love Spiders.* New York: Scholastic,

Parkinson, Kathy. *The Enormous Turnip.* Whitman, 1985.

Paterson, Diane. *If I Were a Toad.* New York: Dial, 1977.

Patrick, Gloria. *A Bug in a Jug & Other Funny Rhymes.* New York: Scholastic, 1970.

Patron, Susan. *Dark Cloud Strong Breeze.* New York: Orchard, 1994.

Patz, Nancy. *Moses Supposes His Toeses Are Roses.* Harcourt Brace, 1983.

Pavey, Peter. *One Dragon's Dream.* New York: Bradbury, 1979.

Paxton, Tom. *Where's the Baby?* New York: Morrow, 1993.

——. *Jennifer's Rabbit.* New York: Morrow, 1988.

Pearson, Tracey. *The Howling Dog.* New York: Farrar Strauss Giroux, 1991.

——. *Old McDonald Had a Farm.* New York: Dutton, 1984.

Peck, Robert. *Hamilton.* Boston: Little Brown, 1976.

Peek, Merle. *The Balancing Act: A Counting Book.* New York: Clarion, 1987.

Peet, Bill. *The Luckiest One of All.* Boston: Houghton Mifflin, 1982.

——. *The Ant and the Elephant.* Boston: Little, Brown, 1972.

Peppe, Rodney. *The House That Jack Built.* New York: Delcorte, 1970.

Petie, Haris. *Billions of Bugs.* Englewood Cliffs, NJ: Prentice-Hall, 1976.

——. *The Seed the Squirrel Dropped.* Englewood Cliffs, NJ: Prentice-Hall, 1976.

Petrie, Catherine. *Joshua James Likes Trucks.* Chicago: Children's Press, 1982.

——. *Sandbox Betty.* Chicago: Children's Press, 1982.

Pienkowski, Jan. *Dinner Time.* Los Angeles: Price, Stern. Sloan, 1981.

——. *Numbers.* New York: Simon & Schuster, 1974.

Pinczes, Elinor. *One Hundred Hungry Ants.* Boston: Houghton Mifflin, 1993.

Pizer, Abigail. *It's a Perfect Day.* Philadelphia: Lippincott, 1990.

Plum, K.D. *Fly Away Home.* New York: Putnam & Grosset, 1994.

Polette, Nancy. *The Little Old Woman and the Hungry Cat.* New York: Greenwillow, 1989.

Polushkin, Maria. *Mother, Mother, I Want Another.* New York: Crown, 1978.

Pomerantz, Charlotte. *Flap Your Wings and Try.* New York: Greenwillow, 1989.

——. *Where's the Bear?* New York: Greenwillow, 1984.

——. *The Piggy in the Puddle.* New York: Macmillan, 1974.

Porte, Barbara Ann. *Harry in Trouble.* New York: Greenwillow, 1989.

Prater, John. *"No!" Said Joe.* Cambridge: Candlewick, 1992.

Prelutsky, Jack. *Tyrannosaurus Was a Beast.* New York: Greenwillow, 1988.

——. *What I Did Last Summer.* New York: Greenwillow, 1984.

——. *The Terrible Tiger.* New York: Macmillan, 1970.

Preston, Edna. *Where Did My Mother Go?* New York: Four Winds, 1978.

——. *Squawk to the Moon, Little Goose.* New York: Viking, 1974.

——. *One Dark Night.* New York: Viking, 1969.

Preston, Edna & Rainey Bennett. *The Temper Tantrum Book.* NY: Puffin, 1976.

Roe, Eileen

All I Am

Illustrated by Helen Cogancherry
Bradbury, 1990. ISBN: 0-02-777372-8

Annotation

We all take on many roles as this book well illustrates. A child tells about the many roles she takes on — child, friend, helper, thinker, animal lover, to name a few.

Innovation

Ask children to think about themselves. How many roles do they take on? What kinds of things do they do? Then suggest that they write about their roles using the frame below. You might also want to see the additional suggestions on pages 12 and 13.

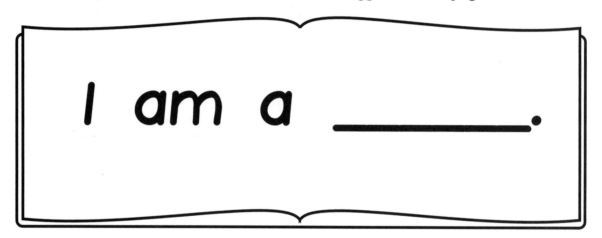

Cross-Curricular Activities

Mathematics: Brainstorm with students the number of different roles they take on or would like to be able to do. Write each of these on a card. Place all cards on the floor in bar-graph manner. Then give each student some strips of paper the same size as the cards used to write the various roles. In turn, have students place one strip of paper above the role if it represents something they do or would like to do. Once finished, point out the likenesses and differences.

Social Studies: Invite people representing different occupations to speak to the class. Perhaps they could show some of the actual equipment they use, and, if they are performers, perform for students.

Rogers, Alan
Yellow Hippo

Illustrated by the author
Gareth Stevens, 1990. ISBN: 0-8368-0405-8

Annotation

If you want to focus on teaching colors and color words, you will want to take a look at this book. A yellow hippo walks along with a yellow wagon and places several yellow objects in it. In a hurry to get home, however, yellow hippo bumps into a ladder, spilling a can of red paint onto her yellow objects.

Innovation

Suggest that children make other color books using different animals. The frame below could be used as could several of the suggestions on pages 12 and 13.

> _____ _____ has a _____ _____
> (color) (animal)   (color) (object)
> to put into the _____ wagon.
>   (color)

Cross-Curricular Activities

The Arts: Have students make a colorful fruit salad. On a large chart, write down one ingredient for each color word. For example, yellow bananas, red grapes, and so on. Shop for each item and actually have students make the salad, reading the ingredients as they are put into the bowl. Then cut the chart apart placing each phrase into a book entitled "Colorful Fruit Salad." This book could be placed in the class library.

Mathematics: Have students use magazines to locate pictures of objects that could be classified into color groups. Each group could be expected to find a given number of objects for each color.

Rogers, Paul
What Will the Weather Be Like Today?

Illustrated by Kazuko
Greenwillow, 1989. ISBN: 0-688-08950-X

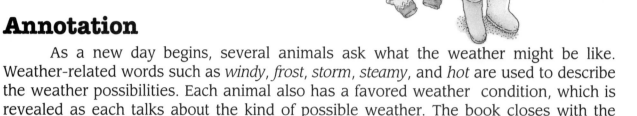

Annotation

As a new day begins, several animals ask what the weather might be like. Weather-related words such as *windy*, *frost*, *storm*, *steamy*, and *hot* are used to describe the weather possibilities. Each animal also has a favored weather condition, which is revealed as each talks about the kind of possible weather. The book closes with the question, "How is the weather where you are today?" inviting the reader to take note!

Innovation

After discussing the weather as shown in the book and as shown outside, have students compose their own weather books. They could choose the animals and the weather conditions these animals would most enjoy. The frame shown at the right might help as might the suggestions on pages 12 and 13.

What will the
weather be like
today?
Will it be _____?

Cross-Curricular Activities

Mathematics: Students could gain a greater understanding of line graphs by creating one to show the temperature for each day of a given month.

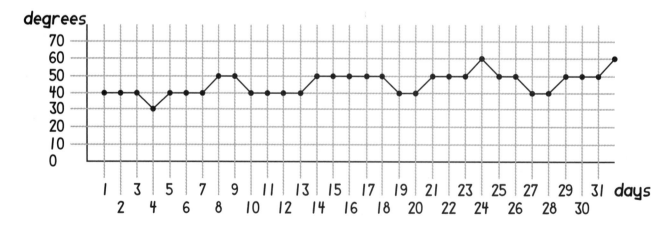

Science and Mathematics: Have students observe the weather conditions each day. Create a circle divided into enough sections for the types of conditions (e.g., windy, rainy, sunny, cloudy). Attach a pointer to the center of the circle. Have one student point the arrow to the observed weather condition. Then, have students record their observations on a bar graph that shows the various weather conditions.

Additional *R*'s

Raphael, Elaine. *Turnabout*. New York: Viking, 1980.

Raskin, Ellen. *Who, Said Sue, Said Whoo?* New York: Atheneum, 1973.

—. *Ghost in a Four Room Apartment*. New York: Atheneum, 1969.

Rayner, Mary. *One By One*. New York: Dutton, 1994.

—. *Ten Pink Piglets*. New York: Dutton, 1994.

Reddix, Valerie. *Millie and the Mud Hole*. New York: Lothrop, 1992.

Redhead, Janet. *The Big Block of Chocolate*. New York: Scholastic, 1985.

Reeves, Norma. *I Had a Cat*. Scarsdale, NJ: Bradbury, 1989.

—. *The Spooky Eerie Night Noise*. Scarsdale, NJ: Bradbury, 1989.

Rehm, Karl & Kay Koike. *Left or Right?* New York: Clarion, 1991.

Reinl, Edda. *The Three Little Pigs*. Natick, MA: Neugebauer, 1983.

Remkieicz, Frank. *The Bone Stranger*. Lothrop, 1994.

Rice, Eve. *City Night*. New York; Greenwillow, 1987.

—. *Sam Who Never Forgets*. New York: Mulberry, 1987.

—. *New Blue Shoes*. New York: Penguin/Puffin, 1983.

Richardson, John. *Ten Bears in a Bed*. New York: Hyperion, 1992.

Riddell, Chris. *The Trouble with Elephants*. New York: Harper Trophy, 1988.

—. *Bird's New Shoes*. New York: Holt, 1987.

Robart, Rose. *The Cake That Mack Ate*. Boston: Little Brown, 1987.

Roche, Patrick. *Jump all Morning*. New York: Viking, 1984.

Rockwell, Anne. *Honk Honk!* New York: Dutton, 1980.

—. *Poor Goose: A French Folktale*. Crowell, 1976.

Roddie, Shen. *Animal Stew*. Boston: Houghton Mifflin, 1992.

Roe, Eileen. *Staying with Grandma*. New York: Bradbury, 1989.

Rogers, Paul. *Don't Blame Me!* Trafalgar Square: England, 1992.

—. *From Me to You*. New York: Watts, 1988.

—. *Sheepchase*. New York: Viking, 1986.

Root, Phyllis. *The Old Red Rocking Chair*. Boston: Little Brown, 1992.

Rosselson, Leon. *Where's My Mom?* Cambridge, MA: Candlewick, 1994.

Rose, Anne. *Akimba and the Magic Cow*. New York: Scholastic, 1981.

—. *As Right as Right Can Be*. New York: Dial, 1976.

Rosen, Michael. *Little Rabbit Foo Foo*. New York: Simon & Schuster, 1990.

—. *Smelly Jelly Smelly Fish*. Englewood Cliffs, NJ: Prentice-Hall, 1987.

—. *You Can't Catch Me*. New York: Dutton, 1982.

Rosenberg, Liz. *Window, Mirror, Moon*. New York: HarperCollins, 1990.

Rosetti, Christina. *Color*. New York: HarperCollins, 1992.

—. *What Is Pink?* New York: Henry Holt, 1963.

Rotner, Sheeley & Ken Kreisler. *Citybook*. New York: Orchard, 1994.

—. *Faces*. New York: Macmillan, 1994.

Runcie, Jill. *Cock-a-doodle-doo*. Simon & Schuster, 1991.

Russell, Sandra. *A Farmer's Dozen*. New York: Harper, 1982.

Ruwe, Mike. *Ten Little Bears*. New York: Scott Foresman, 1988.

Rydell, Katy. *Wind Says Goodnight*. Boston: Houghton Mifflin, 1994.

Schindel, John
What's for Lunch?

Illustrated by Kevin O'Malley
Lothrop, 1994. ISBN: 0-688-13598-6

Annotation

Sidney the mouse decides that it's time to eat lunch. However, his lunch is delayed because many animals enter the scene, each threatening to harm the previous animal in some way. This same pattern proceeds for six animals until Shirley, Sidney's friend, creeps up behind the elephant and shouts, "Boo!" causing the elephants to run home. With all animals home, Sidney and Shirley have a picnic of Swiss cheese and French bread.

Innovation

Suggest that students write a book similar to this one, using either their own names or names of other animals. The pattern shown below may be of help. You might want to have each student complete one page for a class book. Also note other suggestions on pages 12 and 13.

> _____ was gazing at the _____, thinking about eating lunch.
> "I'm going to eat you," _____, said the _____.
> "I don't think so," said _____.
> Because at that moment a _____ _____ up behind the _____.

Cross-Curricular Activities

Health: Talk with students about balanced lunches using the food pyramid. Then have them take a look at their lunches and see if they can find examples of the various food groups. Would they say that their lunches are balanced? Why? Why not?

Social Studies: Lunch boxes and their contents are a big part of school. As a getting-to-know-you activity the first day, have students bring their lunch boxes to the group meeting area and allow each in turn to tell about his/her lunch box.

Stevenson, James

Fun, No Fun

Illustrated by the author
Greenwillow, 1994. ISBN: 0-688-11673-6

Annotation

What's fun? What isn't? This book answers both of these questions as the author tells about his life. Small pictures are used to illustrate each "fun" or "no fun" event or object.

Innovation

Ask children to think of things in their lives that they consider fun and no fun. Suggest that they make their own "fun/no fun" books. Each set of pages could represent a year in their lives. "Fun" and "No Fun" could be written on facing pages. Then, for each year, students could write and draw "fun" things, and "no fun" things. Students might also want to create other similar books such as "Good/Not Good."

Cross-Curricular Activities

Language Arts: Help children to learn about autobiographies. Tell them that when they are writing about themselves, they are really writing autobiographies. Then invite them to share their Fun/No Fun autobiographies with one another or the entire class.

Mathematics: Teach students how to keep a tally. Make a tally for each fun/no fun activity. Once finished, have them practice counting in fives to determine which appeared most often in the book — "fun" or "no fun."

Stolz, Mary
Say Something

Illustrated by Alexander Koshkin
HarperCollins, 1993. ISBN: 0-06-021158-X

Annotation

A young boy and his father go fishing in their boat and talk about the world as they wait for fish to bite their lines. The boy wants to know about many things, and on each page he tells his father, "Say something about . . ." His father provides at least one fact about the animal or object that the boy has mentioned.

Innovation

After talking about the many animals that were mentioned in the book, suggest that students pair up and write their own "Say something" books. They could take turns with their partner. One could ask the partner to say something; the partner says it in writing to be read by the person requesting the "say something."

Say something about _____.

Cross-Curricular Activities

Mathematics: Write given numerals on cards. Place the cards in a bag. Take out one card saying, "Say something about . . . ." Have the students say something that shows an understanding of the numeral.

Science: This is an excellent book to use as a culminating activity for a given unit. For example, if you have been learning about dinosaurs, place all dinosaur names on cards in a small bag. Then reach in, or have a student reach in, and draw a card out of the bag saying, "Say something about . . . ." After calling on a student to respond, that student could select the next card. Continue until all cards have been used.

Social Studies: Write each student's name on a card and place each in a bag. Take one name out of the bag saying, "Say something good about . . ." This would be an excellent way to build students' self esteem and also focus on saying kind things about others.

Additional *S*'s

Satchwell, John. *Odd One Out*. New York: Random House, 1984.

Sawyer, Ruth. *Journey Cake, Ho!* New York: Viking, 1953.

Saunders, Dave & Julie Saunders. *Storm's Coming*. New York: Bradbury, 1994.

Scott, Ann Herbert. *Hi*. New York: Philomel, 1994.

Selby, Jennifer. *In the Still of the Night*. New York: Simon & Schuster, 1994.

Sendak, Maurice. *Alligators All Around*. New York: Scholastic, 1992.

——. *One Was Johnny*. New York: Scholastic, 1992.

——. *Where the Wild Things Are*. New York: HarperCollins, 1988.

——. *Chicken Soup with Rice*. New York: Scholastic, 1987.

Serfozo, Mary. *Who Said Red?* New York: Macmillan, 1992.

——. *Who Wants One?* New York: Aladdin/Macmillan, 1989.

Seuss, Dr. *Fox in Sox*. New York: Random House, 1965.

——. *Green Eggs and Ham*. New York: Random House, 1960.

——.*The Cat in the Hat*. New York: Random House, 1957.

Sharp, Paul. *Paul the Pitcher*. Chicago: Children's Press, 1984.

Shapiro, Arnold. *Who Says That?* New York: Dutton, 1991.

Shaw, Charles. *It Looked Like Spilt Milk*. New York: Harper & Row, 1947.

Shaw, Nancy. *Sheep Take a Hike*. Boston: Houghton Mifflin, 1994.

——. *Sheep Out to Eat*. Boston: Houghton Mifflin, 1992.

——. *Sheep in a Jeep*. Boston: Houghton Mifflin, 1989.

——. *Sheep on a Ship*. Boston: Houghton Mifflin, 1989.

Sheppard, Jeff. *Splash, Splash*. New York: Macmillan, 1994.

Shulevitz, Uri. *One Monday Morning*. New York: Scribner, 1967.

Sieveking, Anthea. *What's Inside?* New York: Puffin Pied Piper, 1989.

Silverstein, Shel. *A Giraffe and a Half*. New York: HarperCollins, 1964.

Simon, Mina & Howard Simon. *If You Were an Eel, How Would You Feel?* Chicago: Follett, 1963.

Simon, Norma. *How Do I Feel?* Chicago: Whitman, 1963.

Singer, Marilyn. *Will You Take Me to Town on Strawberry Day?* New York: Harper & Row, 1981.

Skaar, Grace. *What Do the Animals Say?* New York: Scholastic, 1972.

Slobodkina, Esphyr. *Caps for Sale*. New York: HarperCollins, 1947.

Smith, Susan. *No One Should Have Six Cats!* Chicago: Follett, 1982.

Smith, William. *Ho for a Hat!* Boston: Little Brown, 1989.

Sonneborn, Ruth. *Someone Is Eating the Sun*. New York: Random House, 1974.

Spier, Peter. *The Fox Went Out on a Chilly Night*. New York: Doubleday, 1961.

Stanley, Diane. *Fiddle-I-Fee*. Boston: Little, Brown, 1979.

Stanovich, Betty Jo. *Big Boy, Little Boy*. New York: Lothrop, Lee & Shepard, 1984.

Stevens, Janet. *The House That Jack Built*. New York: Holiday House, 1985.

Stickland, Paul & Henrietta Stickland. *Dinosaur Roar!* New York: Dutton, 1994.

Stone, Elberta H. *I'm Glad I'm Me*. New York: Putnam's Sons, 1971.

Stott, Dorothy. *Too Much*. New York: Puffin Unicorn, 1990.

Stover, JoAnn. *If Everybody Did*. New York: McKay, 1960.

Stutson, Caroline. *On The River ABC*. Niwet, CO: Roberts Rinehart, 1994.

Tedesco, Donna

Do You Know How Much I Love You?

Illustrated by the author
Bradbury, 1994. ISBN: 0-02-789120-8

Annotation

A parent tells a child how much he is loved, using nature to best convey the emotion. How much is the child loved? More than all of the countries in the whole wide world!

Innovation

This book highlights the part-to-whole perspective as the parent begins by stating that the child is loved more than all of the petals on all of the flowers . . . and so on until the parent reaches "the whole wide world" at the end of the book. Suggest that children use the same format to create a book for Valentine's Day for a parent or relative. The title could remain the same, but the objects in the book would change to reflect the child's ideas.

Cross-Curricular Activities

Social Studies: This book could be one of several used to help children better understand their emotions. You could show pictures depicting the various emotions. You could also have children discuss events that make them feel certain emotions. You could also have children divide a a paper plate into sections, label each with an emotion, and have children draw a picture of a face representing the emotion. You could then attach a pointer to the middle of the plate. Students could move the pointer to reflect how they are feeling on a given day.

This book could also be used to help children better understand maps. Give each child a white piece of 9 x12 construction paper. Modeling for them, have them first draw a flower in the center, then make the flower a part of a small garden. Next expand the picture so that it shows a garden within a yard. Continue in like manner until the children have reached a given point.

Titherington, Jeanne
Pumpkin, Pumpkin

Illustrated by the author
Mulberry Books, 1986. ISBN: 0-688-09930-0

Annotation

The whole cycle of growing a pumpkin seed is presented in this book. After growing the seed, Jamie carves it into a jack-o-lantern, saving some of the seeds to plant in the spring.

Innovation

After letting children talk about things they have grown or pumpkins they have carved, suggest that they plant a seed of some kind, watch it grow, and create a book about the experience. They could use the book for a pattern, substituting their names, the type of seed, and the descriptions telling how the plant changed.

_____ planted a
_____ seed,
and the _____ seed
grew a _____ sprout,
(and so on)

Cross-Curricular Activities

Language Arts: Using flannel, create all parts of the pumpkin. Make the parts graduated in size so that each can be covered by the next when retelling the story. Suggest that students retell the story using the flannel board pieces.

Science: Have students plant seeds in clear cups making sure that they plant the seeds right next to the edge. This will enable them to watch the seeds grow. Have students keep a daily plant-growth journal in which they note any changes. These journals can then be used when they construct the books mentioned above. You may also want to create a bulletin board that shows the parts of a plant. Place the sample plant in the center and words for the parts around the perimeter. Use string to attach the label to the correct part.

Tofts, Hannah

I Wish

Photographs by Gareth McCarthy
Four Winds/Macmillan, 1994. ISBN: 0-02-789359-6

Annotation

Wishing to be several places doing and seeing many different things is what this book is all about. What would you see if you were inside a TV? How about if you were inside a hurricane or flying high in the sky? Read this book and discover for yourself!

Innovation

Have children talk about their fantasies. What do they wish they could do? Suggest that they create an "I wish" book using the repetitive pattern shown in Tofts's book. Also note suggestions on pages 12 and 13.

> I wish _____.
> Would that be me?
> What would I see?

Cross-Curricular Activities

The Arts: Have children create a dream collage. Ask children to either make an illustration or find pictures to represent things they dream of having or doing. Affix each to a large piece of paper collage style. Using a dark marker, have students write something such as, "My Dreams" in the center.

Mathematics: Divide the class into groups of three. Give each group a stack of picture cards or word cards that represent the objects mentioned in the book. Have students categorize the words and tell why they grouped their words as they did.

Additional *T*'s

Tafuri, Nancy. *This Is the Farmer*. New York: Greenwillow, 1994.

——. *Spots, Feathers, and Curly Tails*. New York: Greenwillow, 1988.

——. *Have You Seen My Duckling?* New York: Scholastic, 1984.

Tanaka, Beatrice. *The Chase: A Kutenai Indian Tale*. New York: Crown, 1991.

Tanz, Christine. *An Egg Is to Sit On*. New York: Lothrop, Lee & Shepard, 1978.

Tarlton, John. *Going To Grandma's*. Aukland, NZ: Ashton, Scholastic, 1987.

——. *Have You Ever Seen?* Aukland, NZ: Ashton, Scholastic, 1986.

Taylor, Livingston. *Can I Be Good?* New York: Gulliver/Harcourt Brace, 1993.

Taylor, Scott. *Dinosaur James*. New York: Morrow, 1990.

Tether, Graham. *The Hair Book*. New York: Random House, 1979.

Thaler, Mike. *Seven Little Hippos*. New York: Simon & Schuster, 1991.

——. *How Far Will A Rubber Band Stretch?* New York: Random House, 1974.

Thomas, Patricia. *The One and Only, Super-duper, Golly-whopper, Jim-dandy, Really-handy Clock-tock-stopper*. New York: Lothrop, 1990.

——. *"There are Rocks in my Socks!" said the Ox to the Fox*. New York: Lothrop, 1979.

——. *"Stand Back," said the Elephant, "I'm Going to Sneeze!"* New York: Lothrop, Lee & Shepard, 1971.

Titherington, Jeanne. *A Child's Prayer*. New York: Greenwillow, 1989.

——. *Big World, Small World*. New York: Greenwillow, 1985.

Tobias, Tobi. *A Day Off*. New York: Putnam's Sons, 1973.

Tolstoy, Alexei. *The Great Big Enormous Turnip*. New York: Watts, 1968.

Trapani, Iza. *Twinkle, Twinkle Little Star*. Boston: Whispering Coyote, 1994.

Tresselt, Alvin. *What Did You Leave Behind?* New York: Lothrop, Lee & Shepard, 1978.

——. *It's Time Now!* New York: Lothrop, Lee & Shepard, 1969.

——. *How Far Is Far?* New York: Parents' Magazine Press, 1964.

——. *Rain Drop Splash*. New York: Lothrop, Lee & Shepard, 1946.

Tripp, Valerie. *Happy, Happy Mother's Day*. Chicago: Children's Press, 1989.

——. *Sillyhen's Big Surprise*. Chicago: Children's Press, 1989.

Troughton, Joanna. *The Quail's Egg*. Bedrick, 1988.

Tryon, Leslie. *Albert's Play*. New York: Atheneum, 1992.

Turner, Ann. *Tickle a Pickle*. New York: Macmillan, 1986.

Tworkov, Jack. *The Camel Who Took A Walk*. New York: Aladdin, 1951.

Tyrrell, Anne. Mary Ann. *Always Can*. New York: Barron's, 1988.

——. *Elizabeth Jane Gets Dressed*. New York: Barron's, 1987.

Udry, Janice May
A Tree Is Nice

Illustrated by Marc Simont
Harper & Row, 1956. ISBN: 0-06-026155-2

Annotation

This book tells the many ways that trees are nice to us. Udry mentions beauty, leaves, and places for us to play among several other examples to illustrate how much we need trees.

Innovation

Students might like to add their ideas about how trees are nice. Then suggest that other plants such as flowers make our world a better place to live. Invite them to use a slight variation of the title to compose a book about how flowers or gardens are nice. Pages 12 and 13 list some suggestions for individual and group publishing of these ideas.

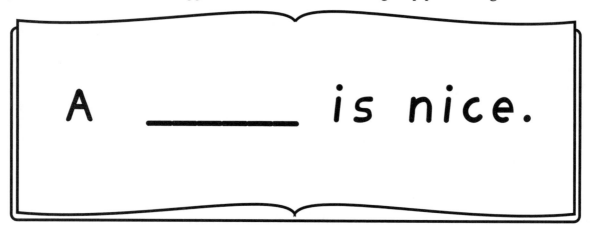

A _____ is nice.

Cross-Curricular Activities

Science: Go on a walking tour of the neighborhood looking for different kinds of trees. Once back in the classroom, create a large tree on the bulletin board and write names of the types of trees around it. You might also want to have children learn the characteristics of deciduous trees. Of course, having children plant and care for a tree would enable them to better understand what plants need to grow.

You may want to bring in several objects made from some part of a tree. Place all of the objects before the students and see if they can guess what one characteristic they have in common. After taking several guesses, tell them that every product is made from some part of a tree. Point out that we depend on trees for many goods, and this is another reason we need to care for them.

You could also bring in a section of a tree trunk and tell students that we determine the age of a tree by counting the rings. See if they can count the rings and determine the age of this tree.

Van Laan, Nancy
This Is the Hat

Illustrated by Holly Meade
Little, Brown, 1992. ISBN: 0-316-89727-2

Annotation

This is a cumulative tale about a hat and how it becomes a home for several creatures. A spider, mouse, scarecrow, crow, farmer's wife, and dog use the hat before it returns to the man with the wooden cane on the same sidewalk where the wind carried it away.

Innovation

Have children recall where the hat traveled. Then ask them to think of other places the hat might have traveled. Suggest that they write about these travels making sure that the hat ends up where it started as in the original book. They could use their own names and own hats when constructing their books. See pages 12 and 13 for more suggestions. The frame shown below might also be of help to get children started.

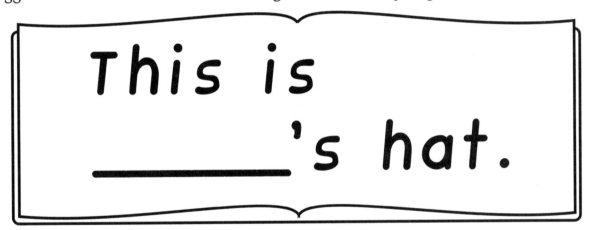

This is
_____'s hat.

Cross-Curricular Activities

The Arts: Have children create pictures using the torn-paper-collage technique used to illustrate this book. First have children think of what they would like to create. Then provide them with the construction paper they need. However, instead of using scissors, instruct students to tear pieces to create their picture. After affixing all pieces, provide narrow brushes and white paint and have children paint around the various objects in the picture.

Language Arts: Draw a circle divided into enough sections for each creature that came into contact with the hat. Have students draw in the creatures, showing the circular nature of this story.

You may want to use the book to expand students' awareness of the word *hat*. Have them name the types of hats and what they are used for. This could be extended to the different hats worn in different countries.

Vipont, Elfrida

The Elephant and the Bad Baby

Illustrated by Raymond Briggs
Coward-McCann, 1969. ISBN: 0-698-20625-8

Annotation

An elephant meets a bad baby on his walk. He gives the baby a ride and takes him by several vendors. He stops at each vendor and asks the baby if he would like what the vendor has to offer. The baby says "yes" to each. The elephant takes each item, which causes each vendor to join the chase after him. Then it dawns on the elephant that not once did the baby say "please." He drops the baby and all the goods. However, the baby redeems himself when he says "please" after the elephant offers him a ride home.

Innovation

Suggest that children use the basic format of the story but change the title so that it names another animal and a good baby to create a similar book. Which animal would their good baby ride? Where would it go? What galloping sound would it make? What would it get? The following frame may be of some help as might the suggestions listed on pages 12 and 13.

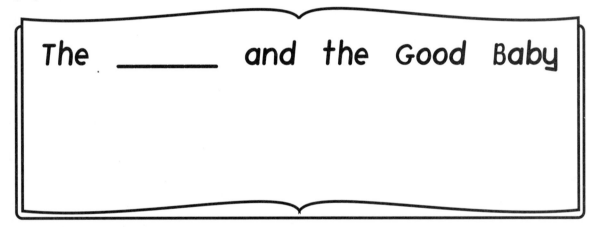

The _____ and the Good Baby

Cross-Curricular Activities

Language Arts: Construct the elephant and all the other characters from flannel. Have students retell the story, putting the characters on the flannel board as they are mentioned.

Social Studies: Talk with students about appropriate manners. Remind them of what happened to the baby when he did and didn't use the proper manners. You may want to generate a list of manners to be used in the classroom. Post the list for all to see and reinforce students when you see them using one of the manners.

Additional *U*'s and *V*'s

Udry, Janice. *Let's Be Enemies*. New York: HarperCollins, 1988.

Van der Beek, Deborah. *Superbabe!* New York: Putnam's Sons, 1988.

Van der Meer, Ron & Atie Van der Meer. *Who Lives Here?* Los Angeles: Price, Stern, Sloan, 1986.

—. *Who Changes Into What?* Los Angeles: Price, Stern, Sloan, 1986.

—. *Who Eats What?* Los Angeles: Price, Stern, Sloan, 1986.

—. *Who Is in the Water?* Los Angeles: Price, Stern, Sloan, 1986.

Van Laan, Nancy. *Round and Round Again*. New York: Hyperion, 1994.

—. *The Tiny, Tiny Boy and the Big, Big Cow*. New York: Knopf, 1993.

—. *People, People Everywhere*. New York: Knopf, 1992.

—. *A Mouse in My House*. New York: Knopf, 1990.

—. *Possum Came a-knocking*. New York: Knopf, 1990.

—. *The Big Fat Worm*. New York: Knopf, 1987.

Vance, Eleanor. *Jonathan*. Follett, 1966.

Varga, Judy. *The Monster Behind Black Rock*. Morrow, 1971.

Ver Dorn, Bethea. *Moon Glows*. Arcade, 1990.

Viorst, Judith. *My Mama Says . . . .* New York: Atheneum, 1981.

—. *Alexander and the Terrible, Horrible, No Good, Very Bad Day*. New York: Scholastic, 1972.

—. *I'll Fix Anthony*. New York: Aladdin/Macmillan, 1969.

Vogel, Ilse-Margaret. *The Don't Be Scared Book*. New York: Atheneum, 1964.

Vozar, David. *Yo, Hungry Wolf!* New York: Pitspopany, 1994.

Williams, Sue

I Went Walking

Illustrated by Julie Vivas
Harcourt Brace, 1990. ISBN: 0-15-238011-6

Annotation

A young boy takes a walk and sees several different animals. He discovers that each animal is a different color!

Innovation

Suggest other actions that they boy could have used (e.g., running, skipping, hopping) as he went by the animals. Then have students create their own books. You might want to have them use the frame below. They could use color words or other adjectives to describe the object seen. Also note suggestions on pages 12 and 13 for different ways to publish student responses.

> I went _____.
> What did you see?
> I saw a _____ _____
> looking at me.

Cross-Curricular Activities

Language Arts: Help students learn to read color words with the help of this book. Give each child a set of colors to correspond with the colors used in the book. As you read the book together and come to a color word, have them hold up the corresponding color.

Science: Have students take a walk around the school (either inside or outside) noting things they see. Upon returning to the classroom, have them use what they saw to create their own books. This same idea could be applied to a field trip and would be an excellent way for children to focus on something they had learned. For example, if they go to the zoo, they could note things they saw using the format provided by Williams.

Additional *W*'s

Waber, Bernard. *Rich Cat, Poor Cat*. New York: Scholastic, 1963.

Wadsworth, Olive A. *Over in the Meadow: A Counting out Rhyme*. New York: Viking Kestrel, 1985.

Watanbee, Shigeo. *I Can Ride It!* New York: Philomel, 1981.

—. *Where's My Daddy?* New York: Philomel, 1979.

—. *How Do I Put It On?* Cleveland, OH: Collins, 1977.

Ward, Cindy. *Cookie's Week*. New York: Scholastic, 1988.

Weiss, Nicki. *On a Hot, Hot Day*. New York: Putnam's Sons, 1992.

—. *Where Does the Brown Bear Go?* New York: Greenwillow, 1989.

Welber, Robert. *Goodbye, Hello*. New York: Pantheon, 1974.

Wellington, Monica. *All My Little Ducklings*. New York: Dutton, 1989.

—. *Who Says That?* New York: Sutton, 1989.

Wells, Rosemary. *A Lion for Lewis*. New York: Dial, 1982.

—. *Benjamin Tulip*. New York: Random House, 1973.

—. *Noisy Nora*. New York: Scholastic, 1973.

West, Colin. *One Little Elephant*. Cambridge, MA: Candlewick, 1987.

—. *Ten Little Crocodiles*. Cambridge, MA: Candlewick, 1987.

—. *"Pardon?" Said the Giraffe*. New York: Harper Trophy, 1986.

Westcott, Nadine. *There's a Hole in the Bucket*. New York: Harper Trophy, 1990.

—. *I Know an Old Lady Who Swallowed a Fly*. New York: Harcourt Brace, 1993.

Willard, Nancy. *Simple Pictures Are Best*. New York: Harcourt Brace, 1976.

Williams, Barbara. *Never Hit a Porcupine*. New York: Dutton, 1977.

—. *If He's My Brother*. New York: Harvey House, 1976.

Wilson, Sarah. *Muskrat, Muskrat, Eat Your Peas*. New York: Simon & Schuster, 1989.

Winter, Jeanette. *Hush Little Baby*. New York: Pantheon, 1984.

Winter, Susan. *I Can*. New York: Dorling Kindersley, 1993.

Winthrop, Elizabeth. *Shoes*. New York: Harper Trophy, 1986.

Withers, Carl. *A Rocket in My Pocket*. New York: Scholastic, 1967.

Wolcott, Patty. *Double-Decker, Double-Decker, Double-Decker Bus*. Reading, MA: Addison-Wesley, 1980.

—. *Pickle Pickle Pickle Juice*. Reading, MA: Addison-Wesley, 1975.

Wolkstein, Diane. *Step by Step*. New York: Morrow, 1994.

—. *The Visit*. New York: Knopf, 1977.

Wondriska, William. *All the Animals Were Angry*. New York: Holt, 1970.

Wood, Audrey. *The Napping House Wakes Up*. New York: Harcourt Brace, 1994.

—. *Silly Sally*. New York: Harcourt Brace, 1992.

—. *Piggies*. New York: Harcourt Brace, 1991.

Wood, Jakki. *Animal Parade*. New York: Scholastic, 1993.

—. *Dads Are Such Fun*. New York: Simon & Schuster, 1992.

—. *Moo Moo, Brown Cow*. New York: Gulliver/Harcourt Brace, 1992.

Wormell, Mary. *Hilda Hen's Search*. New York: Harcourt Brace, 1994.

Wylie, Joanne & David. *A Fishy Alphabet Story*. Chicago: Children's Press, 1983.

Yolen, Jane

Old Dame Counterpane

Illustrated by Ruth Tietjen Councell
Philomel, 1994. ISBN: 0-399-22686-9

Annotation

An old woman chooses threads, begins sewing at dawn, and sews all day and night only to begin again. Her ten-squared quilt reveals all she sees in the world, including people she sees.

Innovation

Review the many things that Old Dame Counterpane put in her quilt that represented the world as she saw it. Then ask students to state what they would sew into their quilt if they were making one to represent their world. Suggest that they write about their ideas. The frame shown below might be of some help.

> For square number
> (give student a number)
>
> (student's name) (some action).

Cross-Curricular Activities

The Arts: Invite a quilter to your classroom to talk about how quilts are made and how the art originated. You might see if this individual would also bring in actual samples for children to see.

Create quilts with the children. Each child could create a square that could then be used to make a class quilt. The square could show any number of things (e.g., a letter of the alphabet, something about themselves, a favorite book). The finished quilt could then be displayed in the classroom or school media center. Students might like to make their own small quilts to tell about themselves or as a record-keeping device for books they've read.

Science: This book could also be used to talk about ecology. What does the earth need? How can we best care for it? In fact, perhaps the quilt square the children make, as suggested above, could focus on something they would like to do to keep planet earth healthy.

Yoshi
Who's Hiding Here?

Illustrated by the author
Picture Book Studio, 1987. ISBN: 0-88708-041-3

Annotation

Animals and their camouflages are explored through the use of rhyme. Each page has a small cut-out section which reveals a unique characteristic about the animal in hiding. Among the many animals shown are a white rabbit, frog, snake, butterfly, and caterpillar.

Innovation

Have students review the animals that were hiding in the text and what gave them away. Then suggest that they create their own "hiding animal" books using the same process as Yoshi. The frame shown below might be of help as might the suggestions on pages 12 and 13.

(student's riddle goes here)

Who's hiding here?

Cross-Curricular Activities

The Arts: Create a mosaic! Have children plan a design for an animal of their choice. Then have them think of the colors they would need to hide this animal. Have them cut or tear paper of the necessary colors into small pieces. Next have them draw their animal somewhere on the paper. Finally, have students spread glue over a small area and begin attaching the small pieces, creating a mosaic. Once finished, students might want to exchange pictures and try to find the hidden animals in others' pictures.

Science: Have students think of specific animals that use camouflage as a form of protection. You might want to list these animals. Have students work in pairs to find pictures that show the animals in camouflage and/or create their own pictures.

Young, Ruth

Who Says Moo?

Illustrated by Lisa Campbell Ernst
Viking, 1994. ISBN: 0-670-85162-0

Annotation

Questions are used to help readers learn about animals. Some of the questions focus on sounds the animals make. Others focus on characteristics such as color, movement, and markings. A review of all animals shown in the book is provided at the end.

Innovation

Ask students to review the various animals mentioned in the text. Then suggest that they create their own "Who?" books. The frame shown here might be helpful. Students could write their "who" question on the front and the answer, in both picture and word, on the reverse side. See pages 12 and 13 for more innovation suggestions.

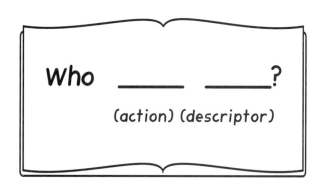

Cross-Curricular Activities

Language Arts: Ask students to write or state additional "who" questions for each of the animals in the book.

Mathematics: To encourage problem solving and divergent thinking, have students classify the animals in some way, letting them come up with the categories. Your only directions to them are that they must have three or four different categories, be able to explain the categories, and tell why they put the animals in them.

Social Studies: If using this book as a getting-to-know you activity at the start of the school year, have students write or dictate a "who" question about themselves. Place each "who" question in a basket or large can. Draw one out, read it, and see if others in the class can guess the person. The person who guesses could be the one who selects from the can. Another related activity would be to display the "who" questions on a bulletin board along with student pictures. Students could be encouraged to match the "who" questions and pictures by using strings or yarn to connect the two.

Additional Y's

Yee, Wong. *Fireman Small*. Boston: Houghton Mifflin, 1994.

Yektai, Niki. *Bears in Pairs*. New York: Aladdin, 1991.

——. *Hi Bears, Bye Bears*. New York: Watts, 1990.

Yolan, Jane. *The Three Bears Rhyme Book*. New York: Harcourt, 1987.

——. *Ring of Earth: A Child's Book of Seasons*. New York: Harcourt, 1986.

——. *No Bath Tonight*. New York: Crowell, 1978.

——. *An Invitation to the Butterfly Ball*. New York: Parents' Magazine Press, 1976.

——. *It All Depends*. New York: Funk & Wagnalls, 1969.

Young, Ed. *Seven Blind Mice*. New York: Philomel, 1992.

Young, James. *Everyone Loves the Moon*. Boston: Little Brown, 1992.

——. *A Million Chameleons*. Boston: Little Brown, 1990.

Young, Miriam. *Jellybeans for Breakfast*. New York: Random House, 1968.

Young, Ruth. *Daisy's Taxi*. New York: Orchard, 1991.

Ziefert, Harriet

Where Is My Baby?

Illustrated by Simms Taback
HarperCollins, 1994. ISBN: 0-694-00479-0

Annotation

If you want to help children learn the names for grown and baby animals, this book is for you. Readers learn about seven different animals as they interact with this book, turning half pages to discover the baby animals associated with each mother.

Innovation

After having children review the animals that were mentioned in the book, suggest that they create their own book or page about an animal for a given category. The frame shown below could provide support for those who need it. Likewise, pages 12 and 13 list several suggestions for ways to have children publish their innovations.

NOTE: You could also reverse this process by having the baby look for the parent. In this case the question would be, "Where is my parent?"

> # Where is my baby?
> # Here is my _____.

Cross-Curricular Activities

The Arts: Invite children to illustrate their books using the style of Ziefert's book. You might want to have students create one picture in black and white and xerox a copy for them. They could then add color to these after they finish assembling them. In essence, this book is a good example of symmetry.

Zolotow, Charlotte
This Quiet Lady

Illustrated by Anita Lobel
Greenwillow, 1992. ISBN: 0-688-09305-1

Annotation

This touching story is about a little girl who learns about her mother by looking at several old photographs. Each page shows a picture of her mother at different stages in her life, from birth to old woman. The closing line, "And this is where I begin" conveys the cycle of life.

Innovation

Ask students to share information about their mothers or fathers. What kinds of things do they do? do they like? Then suggest that students create their own books about a relative who is important to them, using pictures they've brought from home. These books would make ideal Mother's, Father's, or Grandparent's Day gifts. You might want to provide the frame shown below for their use.

This _____
(baby or some other descriptor)

_____
(description of what the picture shows)
is my _____.
(mother, father, brother, aunt, or some other relative)

Cross-Curricular Activities

Science: To help students further understand the life cycle and to recall the order of events, make a copy of the pictures shown in the book. Then have them place the pictures on a wheel divided into enough parts for each picture. Ask children what they think the author means by the last line. Will they go through the same stages as the girl's mother as they grow up?

You might also want to have children care for a plant all year long, taking pictures of it either once each week, bi-weekly, or once each month. At the end of the year, have students sequence the pictures, noting how the plant changed over the year. This could also lead to a discussion of how they have changed over the year. Have they lost and grown-in any new teeth? Have they grown any taller? Have their feet or hands grown? What about their hair?

Additional Z's

Zemach, Harve. *The Judge*. New York: Farrar, Straus & Giroux, 1969.

——. *Mommy, Buy Me a China Doll*. New York: Follett, 1966.

Ziebel, Peter. *Look Closer*. New York: Clarion, 1989.

Ziefert, Harriet. *So Hungry*. New York: Random House, 1987.

——. *Bear's Busy Morning*. New York: Harper & Row, 1986.

Zemach, Margot. *The Fisherman and his Wife*. New York: Farrar, Straus & Giroux, 1980.

——. *Hush Little Baby*. New York: Putnam's Sons, 1976.

——. *The Teeny Tiny Woman*. New York: Scholastic, 1965.

Ziner, Feenie. *Counting Carnival*. Coward, 1962.

Zolotow, Charlotte. *Some Things Go Together*. New York: HarperCollins, 1987.

——. *River Winding*. Crowell, 1978.

——. *It's Not Fair*. New York: Harper & Row, 1976.

——. *The Hating Book*. New York: Harper & Row, 1969.

——. *My Friend John*. New York: Harper & Row, 1968.

——. *Summer Is....* New York: Crowell, 1967.

——. *If It Weren't for You*. New York: Harper & Row, 1966.

——. *Someday*. New York: Harper & Row, 1965.

——. *The Quarreling Book*. New York: Harper, 1963.

——. *Do You Know What I'll Do?* New York: Harper & Row, 1958.

Zuromskis, Diane. *The Farmer in the Dell*. Boston: Little, Brown, 1978.

Sample Text Sets

Listed below are a few of the many text sets that could be created using some of the titles listed in this book. Complete bibliographic information about each book can be found by looking on the page number given for each book.

Animals

Look Closer, p. 97
Barnyard Banter, p. 39
Time for Bed, p. 40
Is Your Mama a Llama? p. 44
Polar Bear, Polar Bear What Do You Hear? p. 64

Counting

101 Things to Do with a Baby, p. 73
What Comes in 2's, 3's, and 4's? p. 18
One Hungry Monster, p. 72
Now We Can Go, p. 54
Counting Carnival, p. 106

Ecology

Old Dame Counterpane, p. 100
A Tree Is Nice, p. 92
What Is Beyond the Hill? p. 34
What Is the Sun? p. 61
I'll Fix Anthony, p. 95

Foods

Alligator Arrived with Apples, p. 31
Hunky Dory Ate It, p. 36
Feast for 10, p. 38
What's for Lunch? p. 84
People, People Everywhere, p. 95

Life Cycle

This Quiet Lady, p. 105
Pumpkin, Pumpkin, p. 89
A Tree Is Nice, p. 92

Relationships

My Best Friend, p. 48
Do You Know how Much I love You?, p. 88
This Quiet Lady, p. 105
I Love Animals, p. 65
My Friend John, p. 106

Working with Others

Elephant in a Well, p. 35
Feast for 10, p. 38
Billy's Beetle, p. 50
People, People Everywhere, p. 95

Questions & Concerns

The idea of using predictable literature can be enticing! Nonetheless, several questions persist, especially from those who are new to the idea of using predictable trade books to teach novice readers. They want, and rightly so, some reassurance that using predictable literature works! Common questions are listed below along with some specific articles and books that can be used to address each. Perhaps these questions are similar to yours.

1. How can I be sure that my students will learn to identify the basic high frequency words?

Bridge, C., Winograd, P., & Haley, D. (1983). "Using Predictable Materials vs. Preprimers to Teach Beginning Sight Words." *The Reading Teacher* (May): 884-891.

2. How can I teach skills with predictable literature?

Cunningham, P. & Allington, R. (1991). "Words, Letters, Sounds, and Big Books." *Learning*, 20: 91-95.

Trachtenburg, P. & Ferruggia, A. (1989). "Big Books from Little Voices: Reaching High Risk Beginning Readers." *The Reading Teacher* (Jan): 284-289.

3. Will my students learn better and more than they would have if I had used a basal reader?

Chandler, J. & Baghban, M. (1986). "Predictable Books Guarantee Success." *Reading Horizons*, 26: 167-177.

4. Can predictable literature be used to help second language learners learn to read?

Boyle, O. & Peregoy, S. (1990). "Literacy Scaffolds: Strategies for First and Second Language Learners." *The Reading Teacher*, 44 (3): 194-199.

5. Is predictable literature a good way to teach children enrolled in special education programs?

McClure, A. A. (1985). "Predictable Books: Another Way to Teach Reading to Learning Disabled Children." *Teaching Exceptional Children*, 17: 267-273.

6. Is there a suggested daily routine I can follow when using predictable books?

📖 Lynch, P. (1986). *Using Big Books and Predictable Books*. New York: Scholastic.

7. Just how would I go about having my students create big books from predictable books?

📖 Heald-Taylor, G. (1987). "How to Use Predictable Books for K-2 Language Arts Instruction." *The Reading Teacher* (March): 656-661.

8. Are there some additional tips I can follow to make sure I use predictable literature and big books the right way and gain the most from them?

📖 Reutzel, D. R. & Fawson, P. (1989). "Using a Literature Webbing Strategy Lesson with Predictable Books." *The Reading Teacher*, 43 (3): 208-215.

📖 Strickland, D. S. (1988). "Some Tips for Using Big Books." *The Reading Teacher*, 41: 966-968.

9. I would like to read more about the shared book experience. What would you recommend?

📖 Holdaway, D. (1979). *The Foundations of Literacy*. New York: Ashton-Scholastic.

Additional Programs

The following companies are among those that provide commercially prepared reading programs in which predictable literature is used. Often the books are prepared for the program. The books are sometimes sequenced in order of difficulty by the publisher. Representative programs follow each listing.

Children's Press
5440 North Cumberland Avenue
Chicago, IL 60656-1494
(800) 374-4329
(Early Childhood Package)

Creative Teaching Press
P.O. Box 6017
Cypress, CA 90630-0017
(800) 444-4287
(Learn to Read Science Series)

DLM
PO Box 543
Blacklick, OH 43004-0543
(800) 843-8855
(Sounds of Language Readers)

Down Under Books
(In USA, distributed by
Ed-Tex 15235 Band Blvd
Suite A107)
Mission Hills, CA 9134
(800) 435-8247
(Eureka Treasure Chest)

Educational Insights
19560 S. Rancho Way
Dominguez Hills, CA 90220
(800) 933-3277
(Giant Step Readers)

HarperCollins (Harper Festival)
New York, NY
(Let's Read Aloud Series)

Kaeden Corporation
3400 Crisfield Drive
Rocky River, Ohio 44116
(800) 890-7323
(Seven sets of readers)

Oxford University Press
200 Madison Avenue
New York, NY 10016
(800) 334-4249

Penguin Group Puffin Books
375 Hudson Street
New York, NY 10014
(Hello Reading!
Easy to Read Program)

Richard C. Owen
PO Box 585
Katonah, NY 10536
(800) 336-5588
(Ready to Read Program)

Rigby
PO Box 797
Crystal Lake, IL 60039-0797
(800) 822-8661
(Literacy 2000)

Scholastic, Inc.
PO Box 7502
Jefferson City, MO 65102-9968
(800) 325-6149
(Hello Reader!, Wiggle Works)

📖 *Scott, Foresman (Goodyear Books)*
1900 East Lake Avenue
Glenview, IL 60025
(Let Me Read Series)

📖 *SRA*
250 Old Wilson Bridge Road,
Suite 310
Worthington, OH 43085
(800) 843-8855
(Voyages)

📖 *The Wright Group*
19201 120th Ave. NE
Bothell, WA 98011-9512
(800) 345-6073
(Sunshine, Storybox)

References

📖 Holdaway, D. (1979). *The Foundations of Literacy.* New York: Ashton-Scholastic.

📖 Martin, B. & Brogan, P. (1971). *Teacher's Guide to the Instant Readers.* New York: Holt, Rinehart & Winston.

📖 Rhodes, L. (1981). "I Can Read! Predictable Books as Resources for Reading and Writing Instruction." *The Reading Teacher* (February): 511-517.

Notes